New Directions for Student Services

Elizabeth J. Whitt
EDITOR-IN-CHIEF

John H. Schuh
ASSOCIATE EDITOR

Supporting and Supervising Mid-Level Professionals

Larry D. Roper

EDITOR

Number 136 • Winter 2011
Jossey-Bass
San Francisco

Supporting and Supervising Mid-Level Professionals
Larry D. Roper (ed.)
New Directions for Student Services, no. 136
Elizabeth J. Whitt, Editor-in-Chief
John H. Schuh, Associate Editor

NEW DIRECTIONS FOR STUDENT SERVICES (ISSN 0164-7970, e-ISSN 1536-0695) is part of The Jossey-Bass Higher and Adult Education Series and is published quarterly by Wiley Subscription Services, Inc., A Wiley Company, at Jossey-Bass, One Montgomery Street, Suite 1200, San Francisco, CA 94104-4594. Periodicals Postage Paid at San Francisco, California, and at additional mailing offices. POSTMASTER: Send address changes to New Directions for Student Services, Jossey-Bass, One Montgomery Street, Suite 1200, San Francisco, CA 94104-4594.

New Directions for Student Services is indexed in CIJE: Current Index to Journals in Education (ERIC), Contents Pages in Education (T&F), Current Abstracts (EBSCO), Education Index/Abstracts (H.W. Wilson), Educational Research Abstracts Online (T&F), ERIC Database (Education Resources Information Center), and Higher Education Abstracts (Claremont Graduate University).

Microfilm copies of issues and articles are available in 16mm and 35mm, as well as microfiche in 105mm, through University Microfilms Inc., 300 North Zeeb Road, Ann Arbor, Michigan 48106-1346.

SUBSCRIPTIONS cost $89.00 for individuals and $275.00 for institutions, agencies, and libraries in the United States.

EDITORIAL CORRESPONDENCE should be sent to the Editor-in-Chief, Elizabeth J. Whitt, N473 Lindquist Center, The University of Iowa, Iowa City, IA 52242.

www.josseybass.com

CONTENTS

EDITOR'S NOTES

Supervisors play a key role in the success of organizations, including communicating organizational values, culture, and expectations. Supervisors are also vehicles for employees' growth, development, and ongoing learning. When individuals and groups receive supervision, they are more likely to perform at optimal levels of confidence and proficiency. Effective supervision increases the possibility of successful performance and appropriate professional development of staff. However, developing the necessary knowledge and skills to become a skillful supervisor is no simple matter.

To develop a healthy perspective on successful supervision, prospective supervisors must begin by developing a healthy view of what it means to be a supervisor. As Winston and Creamer (1998) suggest, supervision must be framed as a developmental activity, a synergistic relationship. When done well, a supervisor–supervisee relationship has less to do with skill remediation or responding to employee failure and more to do with enhancing the employee's ability to function effectively within his or her role. Even more, successful supervision can result not just in supervisees' learning what is needed to be successful in their specific role, but in a broader understanding of how to navigate institutional culture and the culture of higher education, as well as produce awareness, knowledge, and skills that may result in a more sophisticated outlook and performance.

Supervisors can help produce high levels of development by attending to their own learning and embracing the complex responsibilities associated with supervision. Among the responsibilities generally associated with supervision are setting expectations, coaching for successful performance, developing skills, providing feedback, assessing worthiness for merit increases or promotion, and documenting performance reviews. While supervisees come to expect the roles we typically associate with supervision, in many cases supervisees may expect that their supervisor will have sufficient interest in their success that the supervisor may serve in a mentoring role. Every supervisor must decide for herself or himself how far he or she is willing to go to invest in the success of a supervisee. The supervisor must find ways to manage the typical expectations of the role, which are often detailed in one's position description, with the specific expectations that supervisees may have for the role they expect of their supervisor.

Mid-level professionals in supervisory roles often find themselves in a unique position; they are attending to their own professional growth and career development/advancement while also having responsibility to nurture the performance and success of others. In many cases, midlevel supervisors are still cultivating their professional identity and mastering the

NEW DIRECTIONS FOR STUDENT SERVICES, no. 136, Winter 2011 © Wiley Periodicals, Inc.
Published online in Wiley Online Library (wileyonlinelibrary.com) • DOI: 10.1002/ss.408

challenges of more complex roles, as they are being asked to supervise other early-career professionals, office staff, graduate students, or undergraduates. There can be much stress and anxiety associated with negotiating all of the demands associated with being a mid-level supervisor.

This sourcebook was written with a particular focus on the needs and challenges of mid-level supervisors. The chapters blend research, personal essays, personal experiences of the authors, and case studies, as a way to provide many ways of learning about mid-level supervision.

In Chapter One, Tom Scheuermann offers a broad and comprehensive look at supervision. He introduces readers to a wealth of resources, as well as a wide range of issues supervisors might face. Scheuermann offers specific examples of specific challenges supervisors might face during financially challenging times.

In Chapter Two, through a personal essay, Cathlene McGraw gives a perspective of an early-career professional. Cat offers a number of vignettes from her work life to demonstrate challenges she faced and the role mid-level supervisors play in helping her to develop a professional identity and leadership competence.

While we may observe and attempt to mimic the behaviors of others, every person must eventually construct his or her own personal philosophy. In Chapter Three, Delores McNair offers a personal essay that poses questions and provides guidance for developing a personal philosophy of supervision.

In Chapter Four, Mary-Beth Cooper and Heath Boice-Pardee explore the issues associated with being in the middle (located in the organizational hierarchy between entry-level and senior-level leaders). These authors point out the uncomfortable position of being between entry-level and senior-level professionals in the organizational structure and the unique set of skills needed to be successful.

While it is challenging to be a midlevel supervisor, it is equally difficult to be a graduate student employee, as Jessica White and John Nonnamaker illustrate in Chapter Five. Because graduate students must straddle roles of student and employee and the supervisor may also play dual roles of supervisor and graduate advisor, much thoughtfulness is needed to negotiate the role of supervising graduate students successfully. The authors of this chapter draw upon research and experience as graduate faculty to provide insights into this type of supervision.

In Chapter Six, Trisha Scarcia-King departs from the way many think about supervision. Typically, we envision supervision as face to face, where the supervisee and supervisor are in the same location and share daily in-person interactions. Trisha introduces virtual supervision and demonstrates the nuances of negotiating a virtual supervisory relationship.

Diversity and multiculturalism are important and valued attributes of colleges and universities. Supervisors must often traverse institutional and personal dynamics to successfully execute supervisory relationships where issues of diversity and multiculturalism are at play. In Chapter Seven, Larry Roper offers a portrait of the complex issues mid-level supervisors face in working with diverse staff in a multicultural context.

Chapter Eight, written by Lori White, presents a series of case studies that might be faced by supervisors. This chapter demonstrates the complexity of the supervisor role, but also shows the importance of supervisors' developing knowledge and skills to manage employee performance and work group dynamics.

Larry D. Roper
Editor

Reference

Winston, R. B., and Creamer, D. G. "Staff Supervision and Professional Development: An Integrated Approach." In W. A. Bryan and R. A. Schwartz (eds.), *Strategies for Staff Development: Personal and Professional Education in the 21st Century*. New Directions for Student Services, no. 84. San Francisco: Jossey-Bass, 1998.

LARRY D. ROPER is vice provost for student affairs and professor of ethnic studies at Oregon State University.

1

This chapter introduces research and resources that can support supervisors in working with employees during challenging financial times. The author provides a broad overview of issues that are influencing the higher education and current environment for supervisors.

Dynamics of Supervision

Tom Scheuermann

[The] Level 5 executive builds enduring greatness through a paradoxical blend of personal humility and professional will. . . . Level 5 leadership is not about being "soft" or "nice" or purely "inclusive" or "consensus-building." The whole point of Level 5 is to make sure the right decisions happen—no matter how difficult or painful—for the long-term greatness of the institution and the achievement of its mission, independent of consensus or popularity.

Jim Collins (2005)

Introduction: The Supervisory Milieu and Its Challenges

The successful supervisor, like the successful executive, is focused on the long term: decisive, inclusive, and personally humble—what Robert Greenleaf (1977, 2002) would call a servant leader. A student affairs supervisor also is a leader, manager, coach, and coworker. These can be daunting responsibilities, especially during times of uncertainty, with reduced budgets, layoffs, and restructuring. Student affairs supervisors are called upon to navigate increasingly complex educational and work environments and new legal developments, as well as the diverse needs, hopes, and dreams of employees. This chapter frames several key areas and challenges of the contemporary supervisory milieu, including financial uncertainties, the timeless importance of trust, and the influence of new technologies on the supervisor–supervisee relationship. Key references and resources that might be of value to supervisors are addressed.

Supervisor **Defined.** For the purposes of this chapter, a *supervisor* is defined as "a student services professional who has one or more staff

NEW DIRECTIONS FOR STUDENT SERVICES, no. 136, Winter 2011 © Wiley Periodicals, Inc.
Published online in Wiley Online Library (wileyonlinelibrary.com) • DOI: 10.1002/ss.409

members reporting to him or her and for whose performance the supervisor shares responsibility." I assume that, to be an effective supervisor, one must also be a good leader and manager, and supervisors can benefit from the literature and good practices of management and leadership.

Supervising in Tough Times and the Importance of Trust. How tough and uncertain are these times for higher education and student services? The title of a July 2009 article in the *Chronicle of Higher Education* noted with seeming optimism that "Stimulus Funds Provide a Brief Reprieve from State Cuts." At that time, the U.S. Education Department had approved such funds for 43 states and the District of Columbia, which made up for most of those states' higher education budget shortfalls in that fiscal year. The *Chronicle* story noted, however, that those stimulus funds would be exhausted by 2011. Accompanying that article is a table summarizing state aid for higher education 2008–2010, showing the projected change in aid to be either zero or negative for twenty states, and a paltry increase of between 1 percent and 5 percent for an additional thirteen, with only two states (North Dakota and California) showing double-digit increases *with the federal stimulus funds included* (*Chronicle of Higher Education*, 2009).

Keller (2009), in a report commissioned by the Association of Public and Land-Grant Universities (APLU), noted similar troubling developments: "In August and September of 2009, APLU surveyed its 188 member universities about the financial situation on their campuses. Overall the picture painted by survey respondents is dreary, with 85 percent of institutions reporting a decrease in state appropriations and nearly one-half of institutions experiencing cuts of 10 percent or greater" (p. 3).

Private colleges and universities lost considerable financial resources during that same period. A National Association of College and University Business Officers (NACUBO) study showed that 435 colleges had suffered an estimated 22.9% drop in their endowments for the first five months of the 2009 fiscal year (*Chronicle of Higher Education*, 2009). Many of these endowments, like the stock market overall, regained some of that loss in the following year. But, while the national fiscal recovery may have begun in 2010, the psychological and organizational toll—on college and university managers and supervisors, as well as their staffs—will likely be felt for years.

Given the fluctuations in institutional and unit budgets and finances, tolerance for ambiguity will be high on the list of must-have competencies for supervisors in student affairs. The ability to communicate clearly, confidently, and compassionately and through a variety of media, during prolonged or recurring periods when finances and resources are diminishing, is an essential skill for supervisors in student services.

In these times of actual and impending layoffs and budget reductions, *trust*—in the leaders of one's institution, and even one's own supervisor—may be at a premium. Warren Bennis, in his book *On Becoming a Leader* (1989), provides timeless advice:

. . . trust is the underlying issue in not only getting people on your side, but having them stay there. There are four ingredients leaders have that generate and sustain trust: (1) *Constancy*—Whatever surprises leaders themselves may face, they don't create any for the group; (2) *Congruity*—In true leaders, there is no gap between the theories they espouse and the life they practice; (3) *Reliability*—Leaders are there when it counts, they are ready to support their co-workers in moments that matter; and (4) *Integrity*—Leaders honor their commitments and promises. (p. 160)

Supervision

Mission Alignment and Accountability. Given the depth and breadth of financial challenges facing colleges and universities today, Diana Chapman Walsh (2009), former president of Wellesley College, pondered whether we can foster trust and hold on to higher education's highest calling even as our core missions are viewed with skepticism:

> Critics of undergraduate education from outside the academy—as well as advocates from deep within—continue to document a troubling state of affairs. Even the most loyal insiders speak of "underachievement," an "erosion of trust," the end of a "golden age." The major trade associations and foundations are sponsoring initiatives seeking to . . . widen financial accessibility, enhance institutional accountability, and slow the growth of costs. (p. 3)

In a time of increasing institutional accountability, as noted by Walsh (2009), supervisors in student services are routinely asked to "do more with less," while facing heightened pressure to perform and to demonstrate outcomes with data (Student Affairs Leadership Council, 2009). Accountability for supervisors has increased both quantitatively—in the intensity and time pressure to show results and respond to demands for organizational change; and qualitatively—in the complexity of responsibilities including expectations for more rigorous outcomes assessment.

In addition to being financially accountable, today's supervisors need to be familiar with a dizzying array of rules, laws, and constituencies; from collective bargaining agreements and the minimum wage requirements of the Fair Labor Standards Act (FLSA) (see http://www.dol.gov/whd/flsa /index.htm) to the needs of employees with disabilities (see http://www.ada .gov/ for an overview of the Americans with Disabilities Act [ADA]); from increasing requests for family medical leave (see FMLA, http://www.dol .gov/dol/topic/benefits-leave/fmla.htm) to navigating the advantages and disadvantages of growing numbers of "helicopter parents" of the students they serve—and sometimes even the staff they supervise (see College Board, http://www.collegeboard.com/parents/plan/getting-ready/155044 .html). If they have not done so already, student services supervisors should include these areas in their professional development agendas.

Unique Challenges of Supervising New Staff Members. New staff members pose unique challenges to supervisors as these individuals enter into unfamiliar organizations, relationships, and roles. Renn and Hodges (2007) studied student affairs professionals in their first year of employment and concluded that supervisors could "assist new professionals in adjusting to their new environment . . . by having clear goals for supervision, clarifying roles in supervision and/or mentoring relationships, and helping new professionals read the organizational context, especially as related to supervision, relationships with colleagues, and personal responsibility for professional development" (p. 387).

In an effort to achieve a comprehensive understanding of these unique challenges, the Association of College and University Housing Officers–International (ACUHO-I) commissioned a three-year study on *Recruitment and Retention of Entry Level Staff in Housing and Residence Life* (2008), one aspect of which explored the impact of supervision and mentorship. This study found that "Entry-level professionals appear confused about what constitutes mentorship [and] expectations do not always align with the reality of the supervisory relationship" (p. 11). These findings point to the need for supervisors to clearly communicate expectations for their staff members, especially those who are new to their roles. Supervisors should help new professionals negotiate the realities of their organizations, and demonstrably support the supervisee's professional development.

Business Not as Usual, Technology—and Balance. In addressing the panoply of forces effecting change on campus, Iwata (2009) warns that:

> Running our [student affairs] divisions in a "business as normal" mode or thinking that "this too shall pass" without considering new and effective ways to adapt will render SSAOs and their teams ineffective unless more SSAOs can step up and change the way they lead. (p. 40)

Citing Heifetz, Grashow, and Linsky in the *Harvard Business Review* (July–August 2009), Iwata summarizes four key strategies for leaders outlined in the HBR article: foster adaptation, embrace disequilibrium, generate leadership, and take care of yourself.

The strategies noted by Iwata (2009) have implications for the approaches taken by supervisors, including how they use technology. Some supervisors find themselves challenged by being less adept with the latest technologies than their supervisees, and may need additional education and training themselves. Recent developments in social media, in particular—such as Facebook, texting, blogs, Twitter, and Ning—may not be familiar to student services supervisors, even as their staff members and students use these media daily. And although no one can predict what forms social media will take in the future, new developments will surely require additional competencies on the part of supervisors.

Many resources are available to student services supervisors to learn more about technology and its implications for their work: The National Association of Student Personnel Administrators' knowledge community on technology is a good place to start (see http://www.naspa.org/kc/tech /default.cfm). Another resource is *Twitter Power* (Comm, 2009), which provides a succinct overview of social media; and Junco and Mastrodicasa's *Connecting to the Net Generation* (2007) is also an informative text for student services professionals, including supervisors. EDUCAUSE, a nonprofit association whose mission is to advance higher education by promoting the intelligent use of information technology, offers a wealth of resources through their Web site: http://www.educause.edu/.

With work-life balance being a key issue for many student services professionals, supervisors will find themselves dealing with the benefits, as well as the costs, of the potential to be connected to their staff members 24 hours a day. In *Hamlet's Blackberry*, Powers (2010) shares philosophical, yet practical, approaches to help manage this tension between connectedness and balance. "The philosophers," he notes, "offered all sorts of answers, and a number of themes emerged. The most important was the need to strike a healthy balance between connected and disconnected, crowd and self, the outward life and the inward one" (p. 210). Supervisors will need to model this balance and promote a healthy engagement with technology among their supervisees.

Supervision, whether in stable or turbulent times, requires patience and perspective as well as thoughtful, engaging strategies. Supervisory practices that prove effective in tough times should also serve the supervisor well during "normal times" (if indeed one can foresee a return to—or even be able to define—normal times). Before addressing strategies, however, it may be helpful to briefly explore a few key supervisory basics and nuances.

The Basics and the Not-So-Obvious. Following are two of the responses to my Twitter poll question: "What are, for you, the two most challenging things about being a supervisor in student services today?" (April 2010):

"Providing structure for everything and constantly having to reassure them of their performance."
"The balancing/juggling act between support and challenge of those you supervise. And navigating the current climate and demands to operate as a business while still working to create/foster a fun and dynamic workplace culture."

When one reflects on supervision, and the role of a supervisor, concepts such as power, authority, responsibility, efficiency, and teamwork come to mind. A traditional (and rather limited) view is offered by the popular site Wikipedia (2010):

> A supervisor is first and foremost an overseer whose main responsibility is to ensure that a group of subordinates get out the assigned amount of production, when they are supposed to do it and within acceptable levels of quality, costs and safety.

Contrast Wikipedia's superior-subordinate framework with the more complex view of Allen and Cherrey (2000), in their book *Systematic Leadership: Enriching the Meaning of Our Work*, as they note the nuances of supervision and the importance of networks versus the illusion of control in organizational dynamics:

> Networked leadership pays attention to the meaning and forces of cohesion. Traditional hierarchical assumptions assume that policies, procedures, goals, power, and supervisors have ensured control within an organization. Networks do not respond to control strategies; therefore, we need to seek new ways of reinforcing organizational cohesion. The seeking and creation of meaning in our work is one good example. (p. 108)

Supervisors who seek to create meaning in their workplaces will need to find ways to move their teams forward *without fear*, as they lead in a world often *characterized by fear* (see Wheatley and Kellner-Rogers, 1996). How is this possible? One's view of power and authority and how it applies to supervision of staff may be a key. In *The Servant Leader*, Greenleaf (1977, 2002) offers guidance as he addresses old and new views of power and authority:

> A fresh critical look is being taken at the issues of power and authority, and people are beginning to learn to relate to one another in less coercive and more creatively supporting ways. A new moral principle is emerging, which holds that the only authority deserving one's allegiance is that which is freely and knowingly granted by the led to the leader in response to, and in proportion to, the clearly evident servant stature of the leader. (pp. 23–24)

Establishing and maintaining high standards of practice for student affairs supervisors entails working with one's staff to align their vision and mission, as well as fostering relationships across units and departments that will enhance staff development and effectiveness. A comprehensive approach to supervision based on these standards and principles will benefit staff members as individuals and in collaboration with their colleagues. Such an approach will also enhance the supervisor's ability to leverage their energy, skills, and resources in the service of their staff members and students.

Lessons from the Leadership and Management Literature. As one reviews the literature, both classic and contemporary, three major themes emerge to inform today's leaders and supervisors:

NEW DIRECTIONS FOR STUDENT SERVICES • DOI: 10.1002/ss

1. We are in a world of stark, new realities—fraught with unprecedented challenges (does any college or university have adequate financial resources?); and opportunities—what *Wired* magazine in a cover story on the New Economy termed *infinite opportunity* (Anderson, 2009).
2. Leadership at any level, from front-line supervisor to CEO, is inherently paradoxical—what Tom Peters in his prescient book *Thriving on Chaos* (1988) described as "being in control by being out of control."
3. Access to information and to each other across our organizations (and our world) is simple, mobile, and instantaneous. Thomas Friedman explored these phenomena in his book *The World Is Flat* (2005), and Nicholas Carr reflected on their perils in his cover story for *The Atlantic*, "Is Google Making Us Stupid?" (2008).

And yet, in the swirl of these profound changes in our institutions and hierarchies, and the seemingly daily variations in external pressures and demands, lesson number one for managers, says Gary Hamel in his provocative book *The Future of Management* (2007), is: "Principles matter." Hamel's number two lesson is: "The biggest obstacle to management innovation may be what you already believe about management" (pp. 78–79). Hamel elaborates on these themes in an article entitled "Moonshots for Management" (2009), and advises managers to "eliminate the pathologies of formal hierarchy" and "reinvent the means of control" (pp. 94–95). These strategies will require supervisors to act both courageously and counterintuitively in order to be successful.

In these times of intense change and limited resources, can supervisors and their teams withstand the pressure to compromise their principles, given the plethora of practical concerns they face? In their book *Built to Last*, Collins and Porras (1997) answered in the affirmative, noting that companies who experienced long-standing prosperity were able to at once "preserve the core [principles] *and* stimulate change." Indeed, today's student services supervisor must be able to resist the false dualism of principles versus practicalities by recognizing that a team or organization that is principle driven can also be truly successful in practical terms.

With the many pressing needs of today's supervisor, principles and values could seem esoteric, if not outdated. Not according to Tony Hsieh, CEO of Zappos.com, and author of *Delivering Happiness* (2010). Hsieh, interviewed for "Corner Office," Adam Bryant's column on leadership lessons in the Sunday *New York Times*, shared that he and his leadership team developed ten core values, and stated that, ". . . we would actually be willing to hire and fire people based on those values, regardless of job performance." One of Zappos's core values is "Create fun and a little weirdness" (2010). Zappos's "weirdness" value might seem frivolous and appropriate for only a high-tech company or creative enterprise, but it is arguably in the same spirit as the "celebrative" value espoused by Ernest Boyer and the Carnegie Foundation in *Campus Life: In Search of Community* (1990, p. 55).

NEW DIRECTIONS FOR STUDENT SERVICES • DOI: 10.1002/ss

Hsieh and Boyer would seem to agree: supervisors who create opportunities for fun and celebration will be contributing to a positive and productive workplace culture.

The importance of another core supervisory strategy—critical thinking and questioning of the status quo—is becoming more obvious (but no less challenging) than it was more than two decades ago, when Senge (1990) asked in his groundbreaking book *The Fifth Discipline*: "When was the last time someone was rewarded in your organization for raising difficult questions about the company's current policies rather than solving urgent problems?" Senge chided workplace teams for their organizational timidity:

> Even if we feel uncertain or ignorant, we learn to protect ourselves from the pain of appearing uncertain or ignorant. That very process blocks out any new understandings which might threaten us. The consequence is . . . "skilled incompetence"—teams full of people who are incredibly proficient at keeping themselves from learning. (p. 25)

Supervisors need to be confident enough to question their organization's leaders. They also must be open to questions and criticism from their own supervisees, as they determine priorities and foster alignment with the missions and values of their institutions.

Supervision and Embracing the Increasing Diversity in Students and Staff

Demographic changes in student and staff populations can profoundly affect the practice of supervision in student services. Brewer (2010), speaking on "Reinventing the American University," noted that "challenges include demographic shifts, a changing economy, and a declining public funding base" and that "the demographic groups that will show the greatest growth are those that have traditionally been underserved by post-secondary institutions, thus posing a challenge to institutions to expand access" (p. 1).

These changing demographics present supervisors with additional challenges and opportunities in working with their staff members and preparing them to be more effective in their service to students. Brett, Behfar, and Kern (2006) offer this insight on managing multicultural teams:

> Though multicultural teams face challenges that are not directly attributable to cultural differences, such differences underlay whatever problem needed to be addressed in many of the teams we studied. . . . Managers who intervene early and set norms; teams and managers who structure social interaction and work to engage everyone on the team; and teams that can see problems as stemming from culture, not personality, approach challenges with good humor and creativity. (p. 91)

NEW DIRECTIONS FOR STUDENT SERVICES • DOI: 10.1002/ss

Disability issues may not always receive the attention warranted by supervisors, as they work with their staff members on other, sometimes more visible issues of diversity such as race and gender. Resources in the area of disabilities include their own colleagues and campus offices for disabled access services. Organizational and governmental online resources can also help inform supervisors on the basics; these include the Association on Higher Education and Disability (AHEAD, http://www.ahead.org/resources); the U.S. Department of Education site with an overview of the ADA, Sec. 504 of the Rehabilitation Act, and policy guidance for higher education (http://www2.ed.gov/policy/rights/guid/ocr/disability.html); and the National Resource Center on attention deficit/hyperactivity disorder (ADHD; http://www.help4adhd.org/en/systems/legal/WWK14).

Supervision and Staff Engagement: Less Control Can Equal Greater Effectiveness

The temptation during challenging times in higher education may be to seek greater control over employees and to centralize, to issue mandates, and ratchet up the pressure to achieve and produce. High expectations and a heightened level of accountability certainly have their place in supervision during tough times, but *how* supervisors approach these challenges can make the difference between alienation and alignment. In his popular book *Strengths Finder 2.0* (2007), Tom Rath describes a powerful discovery for supervisors who seek to foster the best work of their staff members. After surveying over ten million people worldwide over the period of a decade on the topic of employee engagement, Rath found that "only one-third 'strongly agree' with the statement: 'At work, I have the opportunity to do what I do best every day.'" Rath further discovered that "for those who do not get to focus on what they do best—their strengths—the costs are staggering." In a recent poll of more than a thousand people, among those who "strongly disagreed" or "disagreed" with this "what I do best" statement, *not one single person* was emotionally engaged on the job (p. iii).

On a positive note, that same research led Rath to conclude, "People who *do* have the opportunity to focus on their strengths every day are *six times as likely to be engaged in their jobs* and more than *three times as likely to report having an excellent quality of life in general*" (p. iii) [emphasis added]. These findings should prompt reflection by supervisors on how they can facilitate high achieving, positive workplaces for their staff members.

Similarly, after mining over a hundred years of management science, Daniel Pink, in his book *Drive* (2009), concluded that the leaders and supervisors of our businesses, governments, and organizations need some tough love:

The problem is that most businesses haven't caught up to [the] new understanding of what motivates us. Too many organizations . . . operate from
assumptions about human potential and individual performance that are outdated, unexamined, and rooted more in folklore than in science. They continue to pursue practices such as short-term incentive plans and
pay-for-performance schemes in the face of mounting evidence that such
measures usually don't work and often do harm. (p. 9)

Pink describes the scientific management approach of Frederick Taylor
as an improvement over earlier, more coercive methods, and using a software metaphor deems Taylor's approach "Motivation 2.0":

The way to improve performance . . . is to reward the good and punish the
bad . . . suggest[ing] that, in the end, human beings aren't that much different than horses—the way to get us moving in the right direction is by dan-
gling a crunchier carrot or wielding a sharper stick. (p. 20)

A major flaw of the "carrot and stick" approach, Pink cautions, is that

People use rewards expecting to gain the benefit of increasing another person's motivation and behavior, but in so doing, they often incur the uninten-
tional and hidden cost of undermining that person's *intrinsic* motivation
toward the activity. (p. 39) [emphasis added]

Conclusion

Supervisors navigating today's student services milieu alongside those they
lead will require a robust "toolkit" of skills and a sturdy "backpack" in
which to carry them. The kit should include some tried-and-true hand
tools such as trust and principles, as well as an assortment of power tools
including social media and just-in-time online management resources. Perhaps the backpack that can best hold these vital tools, and that we can
carry and keep close, is *hope*—a genuine hope in the future, in ourselves
and our staff teams, and in our student services divisions and institutions
of higher education. Walsh (2009) (cited above, warning that the golden
age of higher education was in doubt) also expresses a powerful
optimism:

The hope, I believe, is in the possibility that the current economic crisis
could be just the impetus institutions of higher learning have needed to
become learning organizations, engaged in what Derek Bok (2005) calls "a
campus wide process of renewal and improvement." (p. 4)

As student services supervisors and professionals, we are called upon
to shoulder our backpack of tools, step courageously into the uncertainty,

and engage our colleagues and our staff teams in this important work of renewal and improvement.

In the chapter that follows, Cathlene McGraw provides a personal essay describing her journey as a supervisor. In the description of her experiences, Cathlene touches on a number of issues addressed in this chapter, including establishing trust, diversity, and creating environments that encourage the success of supervisees.

References

ACUHO-I. "Recruitment and Retention of Entry-Level Staff in Housing and Residence Life." July 2008. Retrieved June 21, 2010, from http://www.glacuho.org/Default.aspx?DN=b9ec24e3-58a9-4ca1-a1d3-202f86ee6c40.

ADA Home Page. "Information and Technical Assistance on the Americans with Disabilities Act." Retrieved June 21, 2010, from http://www.ada.gov/.

AHEAD: Association on Higher Education and Disability. Retrieved April 14, 2010, from http://www.ahead.org/resources.

Allen, K. E., and Cherrey, C. *Systematic Leadership: Enriching the Meaning of Our Work.* Lanham, Md.: University Press of America, 2000.

Anderson, C. "The New Economy." *Wired,* June 2009.

Bennis, W. *On Becoming a Leader.* New York: Addison-Wesley, 1989.

Bok, D. *Our Underachieving Colleges: A Candid Look at How Much Students Learn and Why They Should Be Learning More.* Princeton, N.J.: Princeton University Press, 2005.

Brett, J., Behfar, K., and Kern, M. C. "Managing Multicultural Teams," *Harvard Business Review,* November 2006.

Brewer, D. "Reinventing the American University." Retrieved June 10, 2010, from http://www.aei.org/video/101252.

Bryant, A. "Corner Office." Interview with Tony Hsieh. *New York Times,* January 10, 2010.

Carnegie Foundation for the Advancement of Teaching. *Campus Life in Search of Community.* Princeton, N.J.: Carnegie Foundation, 1990.

Carr, N. "Is Google Making Us Stupid?" *The Atlantic,* July/August 2008.

Chronicle of Higher Education. Table: Stimulus Funds Provide a Brief Reprieve From State Cuts, March 9, 2009. Retrieved March 20, 2010, from http://chronicle.com/article/Table-Stimulus-Funds-Provide/47483/.

College Board. "Helicopter Parents Reconsidered." Retrieved June 21, 2010, from http://www.collegeboard.com/parents/plan/getting-ready/155044.html.

Collins, J. *Good to Great and the Social Sectors.* Boulder, Colo.: Author, 2005.

Collins, J. C., and Porras, J. I. *Built to Last.* New York: HarperCollins, 1997.

Comm, J. *Twitter Power.* Hoboken, N.J.: Wiley, 2009.

EDUCAUSE. Resources. 2010. Retrieved August 30, 2010, from http://www.educause.edu/.

Friedman, T. *The World Is Flat.* New York: Farrar, Straus, and Giroux, 2005.

Greenleaf, R. K. *Servant Leadership: A Journey into the Nature of Legitimate Power and Greatness.* Mahwah, N.J.: Paulist Press, 1977, 2002.

Hamel, G. *The Future of Management.* Boston: Harvard Business School Press, 2007.

Hamel, G. "Moon Shots for Management." *Harvard Business Review,* February 2009.

Hsieh, T. *Delivering Happiness.* New York: Hachette Book Group, 2010.

Iwata, J. "Leading and Managing Change." *Leadership Exchange,* citing Heifetz, Grashow, and Linsky, *Harvard Business Review* (July–August 2009). Retrieved May 3, 2010, from http://www.leadershipexchange-digital.com/lexmail/2010spring.

Junco, R., and Mastrodicasa, J. *Connecting to the Net Generation.* Washington, D.C.: NASPA, 2007.

Keller, C. M. *Coping Strategies of Public Universities During the Economic Recession of 2009.* Washington, D.C.: APLU, 2009.

NASPA. *Knowledge Community: Technology.* Retrieved May 14, 2010, from http://www.naspa.org/kc/tech/default.cfm.

National Resource Center on AD/HD. *Dealing with Systems, Legal Rights: Higher Education and the Workplace (WWWK14).* Retrieved April 14, 2010, from http://www.help4adhd.org/en/systems/legal/WWWK14.

Peters, T. *Thriving on Chaos.* New York: Knopf, 1988.

Pink, D. *Drive.* New York: Riverhead Books, 2009.

Powers.W. *Hamlet's Blackberry.* New York: Harper, 2010.

Rath, T. *Strengths Finder.* New York: Gallup Press, 2007.

Renn, K. A., and Hodges, J. P. "The First Year on the Job: Experiences of New Professionals in Student Affairs." *NASPA Journal*, 2007, 44(2), 367–391.

Scheuermann, T. D. *Twitter Poll on Supervision.* Corvallis, Ore.: Author, April 2010.

Senge, P. *The Fifth Discipline.* New York: Currency Doubleday, 1990.

Student Affairs Leadership Council. *The Data-Driven Student Affairs Enterprise.* Washington, D.C.: Advisory Board Company, 2009.

U.S. Department of Education. "Civil Rights Disability Discrimination." Retrieved April 14, 2010, from http://www2.ed.gov/policy/rights/guid/ocr/disability.html.

Walsh, D. C. "Holding on to Higher Education's Highest Calling in Hard Times." *Journal of College and Character*, September 2009, 10(6).

Wheatley, M. J., and Kellner-Rogers, M. *A Simpler Way.* San Francisco: Berrett-Koehler, 1996.

Wikipedia. "Supervisor." Retrieved May 14, 2010, from http://en.wikipedia.org/wiki/Supervisor.

TOM SCHEUERMANN, MA, JD, *is director of university housing and dining services, and a graduate faculty member in the College of Education at Oregon State University.*

2

This chapter explores the roles one's personal attributes play in determining one's style and beliefs about supervision.

Reflections on Building Capacity as a Supervisor in College Student Services

Cathlene E. McGraw

My desire to develop supervisory skills was a major factor in my decision to attend a student affairs graduate program rather than pursuing a student affairs position without acquiring a graduate degree. Once I began graduate school, I believed my professors would teach me the necessary theoretical frameworks to inform my supervision. Naively, I thought my classroom experience would teach me theories and provide me with sufficient knowledge to supervise the individual employees and staff groups for which I might be assigned responsibility. Soon, I discovered learning to be a good supervisor is not as simple as receiving instruction. I learned that, for me, making sense of something as complex and nuanced as supervision requires experience, as well as understanding theories of human and organizational development.

Supervision, I discovered, is about building relationships with groups and individuals, as well as implementing policies and practices to create clear expectations. These policies, practices, expectations, and relationships ought to give rise to a work environment that encourages creativity, learning, and personal growth. A combination of theory, opportunities for relationship building, and regular opportunities to apply my learning in practical settings combined to shape my current approach to supervision.

In this chapter, I reflect on my personal experience as a first-time supervisor and share the challenges with which I was confronted and the learning that resulted from my efforts. I describe the role mid-level supervisors played in supporting my performance, learning, and skills as an early-career student affairs professional. This chapter is written as a personal

New Directions for Student Services, no. 136, Winter 2011 © Wiley Periodicals, Inc.
Published online in Wiley Online Library (wileyonlinelibrary.com) • DOI: 10.1002/ss.410

narrative in which I recount key episodes from my professional experiences and the learning I gained from my supervisors.

Early Lessons: Experiential Learning Opportunities

I am running through the hallways of my student co-op to answer the house phone. I am nineteen years old and late for the fourth time to my shift as a lifeguard at the student recreation center. This is my first job, and already it has been a big term for me: my partner moved in with me; the police came to our thirty-student co-op for the second time this term responding to noise and drug complaints from a neighbor; and my grandfather and dog died. It is my first term as a queer student leader on campus and I am often so excited about projects for my student union that I am frequently late to my lifeguard job. I am having trouble balancing my lifeguard job and my student leadership role, as well as my responsibilities at the co-op. On the day I receive a call from my supervisor, I am cleaning the co-op's shared bathroom and have failed to keep an eye on the time.

"Cathlene, we are going to have to let you go." It is my supervisor from the pool on the phone. From the beginning of my employment at the recreation center, when she provided work expectations for the lifeguards, she indicated that we had three opportunities to be late to work. She reminds me that I am late for the fourth time. I am shocked. I start to cry and go through a tearful account of all the stresses in my life—from my dog to my grandpa to the police to my partner. She reminds me of our employment agreement and then suggests to me campus resources that might help me manage my stress and problems with time management.

Though I did not appreciate it at the time, my supervisor offered me several insights into the role of supervisors: she provided clear communication to me at the beginning of my employment experience, explaining her expectations; when my behavior did not meet those expectations, we revisited the expectations; she explained to me the effect of my behavior on other staff members; and when my tardy behavior did not change, she terminated my employment, consistent with the expectations she set at the beginning. During the termination conversation, she made an effort to empathize with the personal struggles I was having. At the same time, she explained to me that I would no longer have a job as a lifeguard, and why. She kept her role as a supervisor clear, as well as the limits of her ability to provide resources to me. Even when I showed signs of distress during the termination conversation, she did not waiver from her decision to end my employment. At the same time, she demonstrated concern for my well-being by providing me with information about campus resources.

This approach eventually helped me to understand that a supervisor must be very clear with supervisees about expectations. She also demonstrated the importance of holding supervisees accountable for fulfilling expectations.

NEW DIRECTIONS FOR STUDENT SERVICES • DOI: 10.1002/ss

Passing Along the Lesson: Expectations of Accountability

Some years later I remembered my experience with my lifeguard supervisor when I called a student worker to my office. I asked my current supervisor to help me have the conversation with her, as I wanted to be clear about the purpose of the meeting and felt the need to have someone with more experience help me. The student worker was in the middle of a messy breakup with her girlfriend and had been unable to fulfill her job obligations in my office. The student and I had had two meetings prior to the impending meeting to address my concerns about her performance. In addition to relationship challenges, the student was working through difficult experiences with abusive family members.

As soon as the student sat down with my supervisor and me, she began to cry, while offering explanations about her priorities. My supervisor helped me explain to her that we needed to make progress with the projects attached to her position and we needed to find a new student worker who could make these projects a priority. We told her we cared a great deal about what was happening in her life and we wanted to continue to be a source of support for her. When the student left my office that day, I remember feeling broken-hearted, wondering if she would continue to use the support services provided by my program.

Three years after that conversation, I had the occasion to chat with the same student via instant messenger. She had graduated, moved to a big city, and was living happily on her own. During the course of the communication, I told her I was writing a narrative on my experiences as a supervisor. She asked if I was intending to include the event when I fired her. It was clear to me that she understood, as did I, that the experience of terminating an employee is significant for the supervisor and supervisee. It also reinforced for me the long-term impact supervisors can have on supervisees.

Impacts of My Supervisor/Supervisee Relationships

Supervisees need support that matches the level of preparation they have to perform their job. I came to understand this when, at the age of twenty-two, I found myself working in an area that I had long coveted—student affairs. My professional development was enhanced by two student affairs professionals who provided me with substantial career-related opportunities. Two student affairs professionals, one in Lesbian Gay Bisexual Transgender (LGBT) services and the other in student orientation programs, provided me with internships affiliated with their national and regional professional organizations.

During these experiences, both leaders assigned me projects to manage that were just beyond my skill level. They set clear timelines and goals and followed up at regular weekly meetings and when I needed support for specific project-related matters.

Both of these supervisors communicated to me very different examples of how one can approach professional roles. Other student staff and I regularly went to lunch and out for drinks after work with one of my supervisors. With this supervisor we shared stories from our personal lives and regularly disclosed information about romantic relationships, friends, and frustrations at work or school. This supervisor and I observed each other cry during moments of frustration.

The other supervisor and I went to lunch only when there were occasions to celebrate. I never saw her cry or demonstrate outward emotions. I knew little about her personal life, though I chatted with her about my life often. When I shared frustrations from other parts of my life with her, she would gently direct me to campus resources to help me with my troubles. She cautioned me to maintain appropriate boundaries in my relationships with students as I transitioned from a student role to one of a young professional in student affairs. She explained that I could expect my relationships with students and professional colleagues to change as I moved from student status to a professional role. She believed I needed to distance myself from friendships with students and learn to curtail my indiscriminate spread of personal information, which was a habit of mine. She warned that appearing to be close with some students could alienate other students. She also told me that there needed to be clear boundaries between student affairs professionals and the romantic relationships of the students with whom the professional works. In her view, the power imbalance between professionals and students is too great to have unclear relationship boundaries.

These two supervisors helped me to understand that the role of a supervisor involves more than just making sure an employee performs the tasks associated with her job. I learned the important role a supervisor plays in orienting a supervisee to standards of professional conduct, providing guidance on developing necessary relationships, and providing insights into the risks associated with one's role at the institution.

In practice, I've blended the two styles of supervision because I believe my role as a supervisor of LGBT students entails some unique considerations. For example, I often find myself in the position of using the same LGBT resources in my community as the students with whom I work. Because our city is small, there are very few options for LGBT nightlife, which means I can expect to run into at least one of the students with whom I work while I am out socializing. Because of this, students see me interacting in my personal life and are aware of whom I am dating or who my personal friends are. In addition, because of the absence of LGBT professionals to serve as mentors and role models, I have decided to share aspects of my life openly with students and demonstrate for them how I am navigating my queer identity and relationships, as many of them struggle with the coming-out process.

My supervisors conveyed to me that a supervisor should work with his or her supervisees to understand the supervisees' career goals and then provide opportunities to support those goals. I remembered this advice when a student told me that she wanted to pursue a career in student affairs. By the time she shared this ambition with me, she had worked in my office for a year. She had been a consistent and reliable employee and a creative problem solver. We worked together to find projects to challenge her. I suggested to her that she read student development theory and we could talk about where that might apply. She tried that idea and did not like it. She wanted something more focused on practice than theory. Our office needed help organizing an LGBT ally training program. As a work project, she reviewed our current materials and suggested new exercises that we could incorporate into our program. This effort required that she facilitate new exercises in front of groups who had never received this kind of training. Her work developing the program eventually led to our office having the opportunity to present a "Multicultural Awareness in the Workplace" workshop to organizations within the National Association of Student Personnel Administrators, Region V.

The midlevel supervisors with whom I worked exposed me to the importance of being engaged in professional associations. Their mentoring was crucial to my developing confidence, as well as to developing skills in designing workshops, presenting, and public speaking.

Having the opportunity to provide mentoring to student workers, similar to that which I received during my internship, increased my feelings of effectiveness as a supervisor. Though my supervisors informed the many ways in which I mentor students in the area of goal setting, their approaches to creating and maintaining professional distance from students have not met my needs in working with students. While I agree with the views of previous supervisors that there is a power imbalance between supervisees and supervisors, I also believe supervisees are more successful when they are able to bring their whole lives to a work environment. I believe the degree of professional distance I was advised to keep between students and me does not contribute to nurturing the work environment I hope to create.

While I was advised that I ought to limit the amount of personal information that I share with and solicit from supervisees, I have not experienced personal aloofness to be useful when students are looking for information to successfully navigate their unique experiences or identities. For example, a literature review confirms that contemporary students in the United States face incredible pressures and misinformation about issues of drug and alcohol use and sex (National Advisory Council on Alcohol Abuse and Alcoholism, 2007). However, while there are many sources of information on campus for risk reduction with alcohol, drugs, and safer sex practices, information on bondage and dominance or polyamory (the practice of navigating open relationships in ways that are ethically and emotionally sustainable) (Easton and Liszt, 2009) is not readily available on our campus.

NEW DIRECTIONS FOR STUDENT SERVICES • DOI: 10.1002/ss

Some time ago, while driving from Oregon to Idaho for a conference, eight students started a conversation about polyamory. The students involved in the conversation wanted to know how these relationships worked in practice: Did all of you live together? What did your parents think? How did you talk about your relationships in class when you were a student? Because I was open to sharing and hearing the experiences of the students, they were able to talk with one another about the experiences they were having in their lives. My experience shows me that students are looking for information that is more nuanced than student affairs professionals have provided in the past. In smaller cities, such as where I reside, student affairs professionals may be the only resource for these kinds of questions. I have drawn upon the advice of previous supervisors and find it helpful to have had supervisors with different work styles. At the same time, as a person at the early stage of my career, it is helpful to have a supervisor who coaches me through challenging situations and supports me in developing a supervisory style that suits my personality and job responsibilities.

Power and Supervision

A discussion on personal disclosure in supervisory relationships can reveal power dynamics between the supervisor and supervisee. Two lessons from my personal experiences illuminate my understanding of power in supervisory relationships. First, when I was pursuing my master's degree, I had a position in the dean of students' office. Within the first three weeks of my graduate school experience, a significant number of people I met told me I needed to meet a particular colleague. By chance, I happened to meet this person when we both arrived at the same time to conduct business with the dean's assistant. He introduced himself, and we both said we had heard great things about each other. He was at the office to sign his papers to become the interim director of LGBT Services, an office where I would intern in the coming months and where the following interaction took place:

"Why would you call us 'your' students? We work with you; we don't belong to you." A group of us were headed to a meeting together, and one of "my" favorite students was confronting me. As a graduate intern in the LGBT center, I help to advise the staff of the center. I explained to her that a former supervisor always called her employees "her" students and that I had looked forward to working with a staff of students of my own. I told her that I'd always experienced the term as a sign of affection. My new colleague overheard this exchange and he asserted that a staff should not be a group of students that I seek to call my own, but, instead, a group of student colleagues with collective and individual goals and developmental needs. He also shared with me insights on power relationships. He talked about different kinds of power: *power over, power to, power of,* and *power*

NEW DIRECTIONS FOR STUDENT SERVICES • DOI: 10.1002/ss

with, a theory pioneered by Mary Parker Follett (1924). He explained that *power of* is a conferred power, as in power of attorney, and that *power to* is a power that I give to someone. What I had just experienced with the student was tension between *power with* and *power over. Power over* describes a power relationship that is characterized by dominance. The student explained to me that from her perspective, I was looking to have a *power over* relationship like a parent has power over his or her children. She said that she preferred to be in a *power with* relationship with her supervisors. She explained that this is a relational kind of power, the kind of relationship where students are colleagues.

The conversation about power helped me think about the type of relationship I would like to have with my supervisor. I prefer to have a relationship characterized by sharing, collaboration, joint problem solving, and open communication. I wish to have a supervisory relationship that allows for mentoring and empowerment, as I know being empowered and mentored by a supervisor will enhance my job satisfaction and success (Manathunga, 2007; Boje and Rosile, 2001). The supervisors with whom I have worked have modeled for me many of the attributes I hope to possess. At the same time, some behaviors (such using the term *my staff*) do not fit well for me.

The second lesson occurred recently as I navigated my experience as the first director of the campus LGBT center. I supervise a four-person staff and a graduate assistant, and share supervision of 85 volunteers with the center's graduate assistant. The LGBT center existed as a student organization for 30 years prior to my arrival; the center became a department housed within the student affairs division in 2010.

I began this experience with limited understanding of the expectations of my position. At the start of my first year, I inherited a student staff that had been hired by the previous advisor. Inheriting a staff had both advantages and disadvantages. The advantage was having a team of people who understood and were a part of the organizational culture of a commuter-serving institution. The disadvantage was that the staff was hired under a particular set of expectations, and I struggled to move them to different expectations I had for their roles. Because the students were accustomed to leading in a student organization, they struggled with the more structured and disciplined environment I sought to establish with the staff.

In my initial supervision of the center, I chose to micromanage the staff. I placed myself at an incredible disadvantage because, rather than allowing supervisees to make decisions based in their expertise, I insisted they follow my recommendations for how to handle issues. Now I believe my supervision would have been more effective if I had trusted their abilities. However, that would have been possible only if I had had the confidence to do so. As a result of reflection, learning, and growth, I am able to supervise using a consensus model that places much more responsibility on supervisees. I am able to serve in more of an advisory role and perform in a way more reflective of our mission and vision. This shift has had a positive influence on how satisfied supervisees are in their jobs and how happy I am in my role.

My new position was LGBT Center Director at an urban, commuter institution; my previous position was at a large research university. As I made the transition from one institution to the other, I relied on my supervisor for help translating the culture and helping me to navigate the campus-specific ways of doing things. For me, the supervisor was a translator and guide, helping me to understand the meanings behind behaviors, while also helping me figure out how to be successful doing things differently. At the same time, I was trusted to supervise the center staff, which allowed me to make mistakes and learn from those mistakes. Supervisors play a crucial role in providing orientation to a position and institutional culture.

Navigating Differences

I believe that some of my first-year supervision blunders came from my unwillingness to translate what I learned in the classroom and from my mentors into practice. I also believe the struggles came from the difficulties I faced in engaging with student colleagues who are different from myself. When student affairs professionals are asked to engage with underrepresented populations or with populations that are different from them, a balancing act may ensue. The professional must be supportive of the student's educational and emotional needs, hold the student to high expectations in his or her job, and be aware of the complexities of identity development as a marginalized student. Marginalized students may not receive valuable critical feedback or be held to the highest employment standards as a result of a student affairs professional's concerns about negatively affecting the student's identity development. For example, at times, when working with transgender students or students of color, I felt confused in my ability to understand and support their developmental needs within our supervisory relationship. I managed to convince myself that a transgender student I supervise wouldn't be able to manage the complexity of issues he faces on our campus and absorb the feedback I want to give him about his work performance. However, after raising this concern with the student, I realized that my fears were unfounded.

Working with this student provided me opportunities to work with ideas, experiences, and people that were unfamiliar to me. From this and other challenging experiences, I resolved that supervisees with whom I work must learn how to effectively engage people who are different from them.

My supervisors have held me accountable for exploring difference and working with students, staff, and faculty who are different from me, utilizing the awareness, knowledge, and skills model. Multicultural awareness, knowledge, and skills are integral to my success in the student affairs profession (Pope, Reynolds, and Mueller, 2004). My supervisors have been important guides for exploring my responsibility to incorporate multiculturalism into my performance.

Drawing on Past Experiences and Looking Ahead

At the beginning of my experience as a student affairs professional, I thought I would learn everything I needed to know about supervision from my classes in a student affairs graduate program. However, I learned that my supervision style is largely informed by my experiences as a supervisee and by synthesizing past experiences and classroom learning along the way. Losing a job, gaining new supervision responsibilities, understanding theory, and reflecting on past supervisee experiences each shapes my beliefs and philosophies on supervision. As I continue to gain experiences as a supervisor, my philosophy and practice will evolve to meet the changing needs and expectations of my work environments, supervisors, and supervisees.

In the next chapter, Delores McNair discusses the importance of having a supervisory philosophy, the need to connect that philosophy with one's specific core values of supervision, and tangible steps a supervisor can take to develop or reassess his or her philosophy and articulate it to others.

References

Boje, D. M., and Rosile, G. A. "Where's the Power in Empowerment? Answers From Follett and Clegg." *Journal of Applied Behavioral Science*, 2001, 37(90), 90–117.

Easton, D., and Liszt, C. *The Ethical Slut: A Practical Guide to Infinite Sexual Possibilities.* Eugene, Ore.: Greenery Press, 2009.

Follett, M. P. *Creative Experience.* New York: Longman Green and Co., 1924.

Manathunga, C. "Supervision as Mentoring: The Role of Power and Boundary Crossing." *Studies in Continuing Education*, 2007, 29(2), 207–221.

National Advisory Council on Alcohol Abuse and Alcoholism. "What Colleges Need to Know: An Update on College Drinking Research." 2007. Accessed September 10, 2010, at http://www.collegedrinkingprevention.gov/1College_Bulletin-508_361C4E.pdf.

Pope, R. L., Reynolds, A. L., and Mueller, J. A. *Multicultural Competence in Student Affairs.* San Francisco: Jossey-Bass, 2004.

CATHLENE E. MCGRAW serves as queer student services coordinator at Portland State University.

NEW DIRECTIONS FOR STUDENT SERVICES • DOI: 10.1002/ss

3

This chapter focuses on developing a philosophy of supervision as a step toward self-authorship. Articulating values and beliefs about supervision helps support our shift from relying on external voices to trusting our internal voice.

Developing a Philosophy of Supervision: One Step Toward Self-Authorship

Delores E. McNair

In *Authoring Your Life: Developing an Internal Voice to Navigate Life's Challenges*, Baxter Magolda (2009) offers guidance to "help adults in their twenties and thirties shift from dependence on authority to the development of their internal voices" (p. xix). Part of developing this internal voice required participants in her study to "decide within themselves what to believe, how to be, and how to relate to others" (p. xix). She further explains that listening to and developing this internal voice are key experiences on the path to self-authorship. Self-authorship, as described by Baxter Magolda (2008), is about trusting ourselves (our internal voice), rather than relying on external voices to guide our lives. As young professionals, we attempt to navigate new experiences based on prior knowledge and begin to distinguish what others tell us from what we believe and value on our own. In other words, we have to decide for ourselves what matters to us, what we believe, and what we need in order to determine how we are going act/be in relation to others.

At the same time, as new professionals, we may find it helpful to rely on external voices for guidance and clarity when faced with new, unexpected situations. We may wonder how to move away from a dependence on external voices when we have few experiences to guide us. Baxter Magolda (2009) describes the three components of the path toward self-authorship as initially relying on "authorities to decide what to believe" (p. 4), then reaching a crossroads where we "[a]ttempt to get [our] internal voice into conversation with external voices" (p. 4), and finally moving into self-authorship where we "follow [our] own vision for how to

NEW DIRECTIONS FOR STUDENT SERVICES, no. 136, Winter 2011 © Wiley Periodicals, Inc.
Published online in Wiley Online Library (wileyonlinelibrary.com) • DOI: 10.1002/ss.411

succeed" (p. 4). Three elements of self-authorship include (1) trusting our internal voice, (2) building an internal foundation by "creating a philosophy or framework . . . to guide [our] reactions to reality" (Baxter Magolda, 2008, p. 280), and (3) securing internal commitments by "refining and strengthening the internal system as it becomes the core of one's existence" (Baxter Magolda, 2008, p. 281). Thus, the path to self-authorship involves separating ourselves from a reliance on external voices, developing our own sense of self, and trusting our internal voice.

As might be expected, this path toward self-authorship can be filled with challenges and may require some guidance: "Moving toward self-authorship requires support for cultivating one's internal voice, particularly until the fragile internal voice becomes strong enough to hold its own against external pressures" (Baxter Magolda, 2009, p. 250). This seems to present a dilemma: how can new professionals move from a reliance on external voices when they may need to rely on someone to support that effort? To this, Baxter Magolda suggests finding "good company," that is, someone to walk alongside you on your path rather than someone who will tell you what to do every step of the way.

"Because we know that adult life demands self-authorship, we all must work toward achieving it and helping others do so" (Baxter Magolda, 2009, p. 16). It is in this spirit that I present some ideas to support the development of your philosophy of supervision. My goal is not to present one right way of supervising or even one specific philosophy regarding supervision. Rather, my goal is to provide one framework that can help you identify your values and beliefs regarding supervision as you create your path toward self-authorship.

Leadership or Supervision

In this chapter, rather than focus on a leadership philosophy, I discuss the importance of a supervisory philosophy. The distinction I make here is that leadership is about the ways we influence an organization, while supervision is about the people in the organization who may report to us. It is about the relationships we form with them, how we motivate them, and how we inspire people to be at their best in the organization. Leadership, perhaps, is optional in that we can choose whether or not we want to lead. Supervision, however, is not optional: we will likely at some point in our career supervise others—committee members, student assistants, volunteers, professional staff, and even executive level administrators.

At the heart of supervision are people: Those who report to us, the people who count on us to help them understand the organization and resolve dilemmas, and those who look to us to help them develop their professional skills. Successful supervision of others requires us to be aware of our own values and beliefs regarding supervision. Some of my beliefs are that supervision involves teaching, coaching, counseling, and advising. It is my hope that these values are reflected here in my effort to be "good company" to you. In the next sections, I describe what a supervisory philosophy is, why having one is important, how to craft a supervisory philosophy, and how this tool can support you on your path to self-authorship.

What Is a Supervisory Philosophy?

My underlying assumption is that a supervisory philosophy is personal. There is no "one size fits all" approach to supervision, and although we will find books on supervision, we are somewhat on our own to articulate a personal philosophy of supervision. Our philosophy is based on our core values and what we believe about the way we want to be in relationship with those we supervise. By this I do not mean creating personal friendships or connections on social networks; I do mean we want to think about the ways we interact with those we supervise. In other words, our supervisory philosophy is a statement of what matters to us: our values, priorities, and the principles by which we supervise others. I also see a philosophical statement as articulating those ideals to which I aspire; the philosophy represents who I hope to be as I interact with others.

The Importance of a Supervisory Philosophy

First and foremost, a supervisory philosophy tells a lot about who we are. We are able to identify what is important to us as we work with others. A well-articulated supervisory philosophy can also help us determine if our philosophy (that is, our preferred way of being in relationship with others) fits with the organization we are in or are about to join. Working in an organization that complements and supports our supervisory philosophy likely means we will thrive. Conversely, working in an organization that does not share our supervisory philosophy may lead to frustration and disappointment. Our supervisory philosophy will also reveal a lot about the way we want to be supervised. Knowing this, we can assess how well our supervisory philosophy meshes with that of our supervisor and consequently cultivate a relationship that helps us be at our best in the organization.

When we identify our core values about supervision, we create a mirror that allows us to reflect on our actions in relation to our values. If I say, for example, that one of my supervisory values is to bring out the best in those I supervise, do my actions support this goal? For example, if I am providing feedback about a report, I might think it helpful to point out the grammatical errors, and I may even make substantial edits so the report reflects well on the writer and our team. If I align this action with my values, can I truly say that I have brought out the best in the other person? Before I respond to the draft report, I might pause to say, "This report needs a lot of work. What action can I take that is aligned with my values?"

New Directions for Student Services • DOI: 10.1002/ss

Reviewing the values embedded in my supervisory philosophy *before* I take action can help ensure that I respond in a manner consistent with my philosophy. Such action is likely to be more supportive and compassionate than simply returning the report to the writer with suggested revisions.

A supervisory philosophy is important because we can use it to clarify what matters to us, align our actions with our values, and assess ourselves over time—all important steps in moving toward self-authorship (Baxter Magolda, 2009; Pizzolato, 2010). The philosophy can be a helpful tool to establish our goals and reflect on our work. Consider again my desire to bring out the best in others. Each year, I might identify specific activities to help accomplish this goal. This could include key professional development activities our team might attend. I can also engage those I supervise in the conversation, ask them what I might do as a supervisor to help them be their best, and create specific commitments with them to support their goals. Throughout the year, I can then enter into conversations with those I supervise to see how we are doing in relation to our commitments. I can also spend time in personal reflection to identify my progress toward meeting my goals and areas of congruence between my values and actions. Because my supervisory philosophy represents values I hold and goals to which I aspire, time spent in reflection will reveal moments when I might fall short as well as those moments when I excel. Such reflection allows me to develop my internal voice to identify ways to strengthen the connection between my actions and my values.

As an assessment tool, a supervisory philosophy can provide a time, perhaps coinciding with our annual evaluation, when we reexamine our philosophy. We can ask others to provide feedback about their interactions with or observations of us to determine how we are perceived by others in relation to our supervisory philosophy. Due to the inherent power differences in the relationship, providing feedback to one's supervisor takes trust in the relationship: we need to trust that those we supervise will offer supportive, meaningful feedback, and those we supervise need to trust that honest feedback truly is desired. If we have taken steps throughout the year to articulate our supervisory philosophy, work with our team members, and cultivate positive relationships, trust has likely developed through that process. At the same time, those who report to us may perceive themselves in a vulnerable position, uncertain about the consequences of providing feedback. As supervisors, we need to cultivate opportunities for those around us to provide feedback with impunity. One way we can do this is to risk being vulnerable ourselves by honestly sharing when we may have fallen short, coupled with ideas for how we might move forward.

Defining Your Supervisory Philosophy

We have looked at what a supervisory philosophy is and why it is important; you may be wondering how to go about articulating our supervisory philosophy. Where do we start? I advocate for keeping it simple. Just like a mission statement, you want your philosophy to be easy to remember, easy to communicate, and easy to understand. Keeping the philosophical statement simple also makes it easier to ask ourselves, "Am I acting in congruence with my philosophy and values?" If our philosophical statement is too long or too complex, the best we might be able to answer is, "I think I am." If our statement is simple and clear, we can quickly determine if our actions and values are aligned in this moment—and if they are not, how we might make an adjustment to create alignment.

Identifying Good Supervision. Because our supervisory philosophy helps define our values and how we want to be in relationship with others, it is important to give its articulation careful thought and attention. To begin the process of developing a supervisory philosophy, you may find it helpful to describe what good supervision looks like to you. You can consider this both from your perspective as a supervisor and from one who is supervised by another. How do you want a supervisor to interact with you? How do you want a supervisor to provide feedback and support your professional development? Is this consistent with how you want to interact with others? The answers to these questions can provide insight into things that matter most to you and identify those around you who seem to share these values.

As you look at others who seem to act in ways that are compatible with your values, you can ask yourself what they do that resonates with you. What values about supervision do they seem to hold? As a next step, you may want to interview these role models to ask about their supervisory philosophy. When you review the results of the interviews, you may notice certain themes and values begin to surface. You can reflect on which, if any, of these values you share. Consider making a list of those values and then see if you hold values about supervision that may be missing from the list. You may find it helpful to enlist the support of a colleague or mentor to help uncover values you bring to supervision that may not be self-evident. For example, a colleague or a mentor might observe a "value in action" (that is, a behavior) that is such a part of who you are, you may not realize its impact.

How You Act with Others. Once you have compiled a list of your values and attributes of good supervision, you can identify your priorities for working with others and the principles by which you act. The values, priorities, and principles can form the foundation of your supervisory philosophy. Your next step can be to turn these lists into statements of purpose. Although your philosophy of supervision may represent the ideals to which you aspire, it may be helpful to write your philosophy in the present tense rather than the future. Writing in the present tense helps affirm who you are today. You may consider writing a separate statement about where you hope to be in the future. For the purpose of articulating your philosophy of supervision, if you focus on who you are now, you can begin to see your strengths and develop initial trust in your internal voice. Even if you discover that you still rely on external voices to shape your work, this important discovery marks a starting point on your journey. It can serve as a catalyst to challenge you to sort through external voices to discover your internal voice.

There is no right or wrong way to write your philosophical statement. Because your philosophy is personal, you may decide to keep the information private. You may want to write it in a journal or other personal document and refer to it at key points throughout the year. You may prefer to prepare your statement as a more public statement, something you post in a visible location—a reminder each day of your commitments. You may choose something graphic (such as a collage or drawing) to visually illustrate your philosophy. What is important is not the format of the philosophical statement, but what the statement says about you and your beliefs. A statement that summarizes your values and encourages you to continue acting in ways that support those values reinforces your notion of self (Pizzolato, 2010). And on those days when you might fall short of your ideals, the philosophical statement can get you back on your true path.

The Evolving Philosophy

Our philosophy of supervision is likely to change over time, as it will be influenced by professional experiences, those around us, and our evolution toward self-authorship. Spending time each year reflecting on and reconsidering our supervisory philosophy can help identify people and events that influence the development of our philosophy. Earlier in my career, my supervisory philosophy was more about pushing people to excel rather than supporting them in their developmental process. Today, I see my role as a guide to help others along their journey so they acquire the skills to be at their best. I can attribute this change in philosophical perspective directly to experiences with two mentors who spent time nurturing my professional development and giving me space to be at my best. I can also attribute the change to prior professional experiences, those moments when I realized that my actions may not have been aligned with my values, as well as those moments of pure joy when my values, principles, priorities, and actions were in complete harmony. Finally, I can attribute the changes in my own journey toward self-authorship to learning to trust my internal voice, which suggested that supervision could be based on an ethic of care rather than an ethic of fear.

Getting Started

This section pulls together the recommendations outlined earlier to provide a set of steps you might follow to develop or revisit your values about supervision. You can design these activities as individual experiences, or you can involve others in the process. Do what seems to work best for you, though I encourage you to move outside of your comfort zone as you work through the steps. Soliciting feedback from others will provide valuable insight that is not always available when we reflect on our own. At the same time, personal reflection is necessary to help articulate what matters to us and honestly assess the congruence between our values and our actions.

The following steps are a starting point. They are designed to provide opportunities to engage with others, as well as time for personal reflection.

1. Describe what good supervision looks like to you. What are the values, principles, and priorities that are part of good supervision?
   - Write an example of when you have demonstrated these characteristics and values.
   - Describe a time when someone else has demonstrated these characteristics and values.
2. Identify three to four people you describe as good supervisors.
   - What makes them good supervisors?
   - What do they do that resonates with you?
   - What values about supervision do they seem to hold?
3. Conduct interviews.
   - Conduct interviews with the supervisors identified above.
   - Ask about their values and principles in relation to supervision.
   - Identify themes that emerge from these interviews.
4. Clarify your values about supervision.
   - Using the themes that emerge from the interviews, identify which values you share. Identify values you hold that may be missing from the list. Identify the five values that are most important to you.
   - Work with a colleague or mentor to reflect on your values and to consider how you might turn those values into a philosophy of supervision.
5. Write your statement.
   - Begin the process of writing your philosophy of supervision. There is no right or wrong way to do this; just start writing and see how your statement emerges.

From Idea to Practice

Once you have developed your initial supervisory philosophy, it is time to put it into action. Consider how you might use it as part of your professional development or your annual evaluation process. Revisit it each year to think about events and experiences that may have shaped your philosophy; what, during the past year, truly exemplified your supervisory philosophy; and what goals you have for the coming year that will allow you to continue to thrive as a supervisor.

New Directions for Student Services • DOI: 10.1002/ss

As we continue our professional development as supervisors, we are influenced by our experience, the people around us, and even the professional associations to which we belong. In the beginning of our careers, we may be concerned about accomplishing specific tasks in the organization in order to build our skills, develop competencies, and become a part of the larger student affairs profession. When we move into different positions, our perspective gradually shifts as we look more broadly at the organization. In addition, as we assume more responsibility within an organization and our profession, we assume a greater responsibility to nurture the next generation of student affairs professionals through our supervisory efforts. If we are clear about our supervisory philosophy, and thus rely on our internal voice to articulate our values and beliefs, we are better positioned to become "good company" to others on their path to self-authorship, thus ensuring both sustainability and vitality in our profession.

In the next chapter, Mary-Beth Cooper and Heath Boice-Pardee explore what life is like for midlevel supervisors. Their chapter demonstrates the importance of having a clear personal philosophy of supervision in order to navigate the challenges associated with being situated in the middle of the organization.

REFERENCES

Baxter Magolda, M. B. "Three Elements of Self-Authorship." *Journal of College Student Development*, 2008, *49*(4), 269–284.

Baxter Magolda, M. B. *Authoring Your Life: Developing Your Internal Voice to Navigate Life's Challenges*. Sterling, Va.: Stylus, 2009.

Pizzolato, J. E. "What Is Self-Authorship? A Theoretical Exploration of the Concept." In M. B. Baxter Magolda, E. G. Creamer, and P. S. Meszaros (eds.), *Development and Assessment of Self-Authorship: Exploring the Concept Across Cultures*. Sterling, Va.: Stylus, 2010.

DELORES E. MCNAIR joined the faculty of the Benerd School of Education at the University of the Pacific in fall 2006. Prior to becoming a faculty member, she served in classified and administrative positions in the California community colleges. She received her doctorate in community college leadership from Oregon State University.

4

This chapter outlines the middle manager's role in relation to common sources of conflict within student affairs.

Managing Conflict from the Middle

Mary-Beth Cooper, Heath Boice-Pardee

In 2009, leaders representing two professional associations in student affairs, the American College Personnel Association (ACPA–College Student Educators International) and the National Association of Student Personnel Administrators (NASPA–Student Affairs Administrators in Higher Education), came together in a joint task force to establish professional competencies for student affairs professionals. Although the task force's recommendations were not wholly endorsed by the membership of ACPA and NASPA, the competencies identified remain relevant.

In its final iteration, the joint task force report outlines ten competency areas for the student affairs profession. Each area begins with a general definition of the competency and provides related knowledge, skills, and attitudes that student affairs practitioners are expected to demonstrate in their roles (ACPA/NASPA, 2010, p. 5). The largest, and perhaps most significant, of the ten competencies outlined is Human and Organizational Resources, which encompasses recruitment, selection, supervision, and evaluation of staff; conflict resolution and management of the politics of organizational discourse; and strategies for resource allocation. Specifically stated in the skill areas for this competency are key opportunities for success for student affairs practitioners at every level of an organization.

Among the advanced skills identified in the Human and Organizational Resources competency is that professionals should "manage conflict at a level of complexity where multiple entities are often at odds with each other and lead groups to effective and fair resolutions" (ACPA/NASPA, 2010, p. 15). Not only does this appear to be an arduous task, but it seems nearly impossible to accomplish in the context of the nebulous and often

New Directions for Student Services, no. 136, Winter 2011 © Wiley Periodicals, Inc.
Published online in Wiley Online Library (wileyonlinelibrary.com) • DOI: 10.1002/ss.412

turbulent position held by "the middle manager" that exists in virtually every complex organization.

Certainly, conflict is inevitable in any multifaceted organization given competing institutional goals, resources, and demands. Although at one time conflict within an organization was viewed as a result of a management deficiency, it is now understood as unavoidable (Frunzi and Halloran, 1991). Supervision, change, and understanding the political landscape of higher education are among the many causes for conflict. Middle managers, defined here as individuals who hold professional positions between front-line professionals and senior leaders, often play a particularly precarious and important role in managing challenging workplace situations. The goal of this chapter is to discuss the key issues facing middle managers in higher education when coping with conflict.

Conflict and the Middle Manager's Role

According to Mather, Bryan, and Faulkner (2009), although midlevel managers comprise the majority of staff in student affairs organizations, they are often the least prepared to manage workplace conflict because of limited training and orientation opportunities. In fact, Mills (2000) asserts that middle managers are largely responsible for their own professional growth and development. When discussing conflict management from the middle manager's perspective, it is vital to identify some of the unique characteristics associated with the midlevel manager.

Clegg and McAuley (2005), Mather and colleagues (2009), and Mills (2000) highlight the complexities of the middle manager role. Literature discussing the middle manager shows how this unique role has been viewed over time. The middle manager has been categorized as "representing core organizational values," to being a "self-interested agent of control," a "corporate bureaucrat," and even a "repository" of institutional history with limited authority or influence (Clegg & McAuley, 2005, p. 22). Although often viewed as pivotal in an organization, the middle manager position encompasses great complexity. Scott (2000) identifies a wide range of skills that middle managers should possess, including fiscal management, professional staff supervision, conflict resolution, ability to advise student leaders, career mobility, visioning, networking, and more. Mills (2000) states that middle managers must communicate both up and down the organizational ladder, often representing their own functional area, while also being versed in institutional vision and perspectives. As Mather and colleagues (2009) contend, orienting middle managers to organizational complexities and political and supervisory landmines is essential to their success. While it may be impossible to address all of the potential issues that middle managers will encounter in higher education, the following circumstances are vital for all middle managers to consider.

NEW DIRECTIONS FOR STUDENT SERVICES • DOI: 10.1002/ss

Conflict Deconstructed. Given the many facets of a middle manager's job, conflict is inevitable. As such, it is vital that middle managers possess strong conflict management skills. As Mills (2000) discusses, middle managers may expect conflict to arise in staff supervision, ambiguity over their authoritative reach, and managing competing goals. Among the competencies outlined in the ACPA and NASPA joint task force report, several key competencies are identified that require conflict management skills (ACPA/NASPA, 2010), including supervision, responding to campus crises, motivating staff, and allocating resources. Middle managers must become adept at mediating differences between and among staff, students, and faculty, as well as other institutional constituents. To gain, or enhance, conflict management skills, middle managers must be vigilant in identifying appropriate supervisory support or training programs, either on or off campus.

Conflict Related to Fiscal Management. Frunzi and Halloran (1991) assert that the allocation and management of fiscal resources is one of the common sources of conflict in the workplace. During the budget process, managers have to make an argument or justification for the allocation and utilization of funds. During this process, middle managers can find themselves in the unenviable position of interpreting the expressed or perceived needs of staff and students whom they supervise while regarding the process and decisions made by senior leadership. Mills (2000) notes that middle managers must adapt to changing institutional priorities, while identifying ways to share fiscal decisions with staff and determining alternate sources of funding. In these instances, the middle manager often plays the role of "messenger," sharing with staff and students senior leaders' decisions regarding programs and services that have or have not been funded.

According to Mather and colleagues (2009), "one of the most important and formidable challenges of midlevel staff is dissecting the big picture as communicated from the upper administration, and delivering clear and concrete messages to front-line staff members" (p. 244). A middle manager's skill at understanding institutional priorities, as well as the ability to communicate them successfully, will likely have a positive impact on the way staff and students feel about an institution or organization. For example, for middle managers, although the specific reasons for particular budget allocations may not always be apparent, recognition of other needs both in and outside of the student affairs division is vital. The ability to communicate the broader perspective of an institution's budget process and needs to staff and students whom the middle manager supervises can also ease, but not always eliminate, disappointment. According to Frunzi and Halloran (1991), if a manager can communicate that a specific action is for the betterment of the organization, "everyone wins" (p. 424).

Conflict Related to Strategic Visioning and Goals. In any large organization, agreeing on vision and goals can be challenging. With limited authority, middle managers often find themselves competing with other middle managers to get new programs approved, or to maintain existing programs and services. For example, the Department of Orientation may want to expand the duration of orientation assistant training, at a time when residence life and housing do not feel that they have the flexibility to offer additional on-campus housing. Such situations can create conflicts among middle managers and their staffs, perhaps leading to a divide within a student affairs division as a whole.

When managing conflicts related to the visionary distribution and use of resources, middle managers must maintain a wider institutional perspective as well as a divisional focus. It is essential for mid-level managers to become adept at understanding all divisional goals, and demonstrate willingness to compromise when dealing with decisions. Although certain instances may warrant a middle manager's going to senior leadership to argue one specific budgetary decision over another, this tactic might impact the middle manager's intradivisional relationships negatively and should be considered a last resort. Regardless of whose budget request gets funded, a middle manager will be most successful by being transparent with peers about departmental requests and collaborative with institutional dollars received. This spirit of partnership can lessen hard feelings and diminish opportunities for conflict.

Conflict Related to Supervision. The ability to supervise a staff successfully is one of the greatest marks of achievement for a middle manager (Mills, 2000) and one of the most difficult. Middle managers frequently assume the stressful role of ringmaster, trying to manage, motivate, and mediate a team of staff and students with multiple goals and personalities. For some middle managers, the ability to delegate responsibility to a staff member is challenging. For others, confronting a staff member's or student's inappropriate behavior is difficult. In all cases, it is important for middle managers to recognize the latitude of authority that they possess; understand that they do not need to have all the answers; and recognize that they will make errors. Therefore, senior management should provide adequate training opportunities and support for middle managers.

At the same time, due to scheduling conflicts, disinterest, or lack of skill or awareness, supervisors may not always be dependable in providing middle managers with the coaching and support that they need. As such, it is essential that middle managers ask questions and establish relationships with other campus resources, including human resources and legal counsel, in order to make supervisory decisions that will be consistent with policy and decrease legal risk. Middle managers must possess impeccable communication skills and the ability to network around campus to widen their support system and strengthen their supervisory skills. Middle managers also must understand campus policies, procedures, and resources, as well as have the ability to mediate and offer constructive feedback to staff. All of these skills are essential to help the middle manager deal with conflict in supervisory situations.

When issues of tension or conflict arise in human resource situations, middle managers may struggle with supervising difficult or unmotivated staff and may not know how best to proceed. A strong relationship with partners in the institution's human resource department is critical for successful resolution of conflicts *before* they become crisis situations. In preparation for this chapter, a human resource director at a large private university was asked, "When should managers involve human resources in personnel matters?" Her response was, "Early and often." Although a glib response, there is insight to be gleaned from this advice. Clear communication with employees, transparent practices and policies, and establishing a regular feedback loop with staff all build employee satisfaction, which is paramount to keeping conflict to a minimum.

There are times when involving human resources is not a sufficient means to solve employee problems. Employees come to the workplace with personal problems that might inhibit their ability to focus on their job responsibilities. Such issues are resolved most effectively with assistance from a professional behavioral health counselor and should not be addressed by the middle manager alone. Many institutions provide employees with a confidential employee assistance plan (EAP), which works with the employee to address the problems that he or she may be facing. This benefit provides critical assistance for the emotional and mental health of the employee, can make a significant difference in the lives of their families, and provides for a healthier workplace.

Conflict Related to Legal Threats. While some conflicts can be resolved using internal resources, it appears that the trend of disgruntled employees turning to legal counsel to resolve differences is on the rise. In *The Trials of Academe: The New Era of Campus Litigation*, Gajda (2009) examines the impact of academic disputes in court and suggests that colleges find ways to defuse disputes before they evolve into legal complaints. In general, middle managers should be familiar with, and engage, university human resource personnel, ombudspersons, or other professionals trained in mediation or conflict resolution before employing costly legal counsel. This might differ by institution, however.

Middle managers might be faced with disgruntled parents or students who threaten legal action. Institutional leaders at every level often find it necessary to seek some form of advice or counsel in dealing with difficult people who threaten lawsuits. When leaders receive the threat of a lawsuit, a formal correspondence or communication from an attorney's office such as a subpoena, or other communication such as a fax or phone call from a law office, they must contact their supervisor, human resource office, or internal legal counsel as soon as possible. Each institution has its own protocol on these matters, but middle managers must seek the necessary support and guidance on issues of this magnitude.

Leveraging Authority to Resolve Conflict

Although a middle manager might perceive that he or she lacks authority (Clegg & McAuley, 2005), the level of influence from first-line manager to middle manager increases substantially over time (Dunnette, Kraut, Pedigo, and McKenna, 2005). Citing an earlier study, Dunnette and colleagues (2005) note that middle managers see "managing group performance" and "representing staff" as important functions of the middle manager position. Regardless of their position in the structure of an organization, middle managers hold a sound and important place in an institution; this should not be overlooked.

To be most effective, middle managers should be *visible* in all aspects of their work, known by students, faculty, and staff for their expertise, and seen as a critical component within an institution's structure. By serving a campus in this wider context, middle managers make essential allies from across the institution, who can assist when conflict arises.

Professional Growth from Conflict

In 1949, *The Student Personnel Point of View* suggested that "personnel specialists as well as personnel administrators should be chosen for their personal and professional competence to discharge their responsibilities" (American Council on Higher Education, 1949). This spirit of professional empowerment, however, has not come to fruition for the middle manager in student affairs. The role of middle manager has been fraught with ambiguity throughout the history of higher education (Mills, 2000).

Within the past decade, a growing number of scholars and practitioners have attempted to address the challenges associated with positions of middle management (Dunnette et al., 2005). The overarching challenge for middle managers that emerges in the literature is the complexity of the role. Some middle managers find themselves serving as a circus ringmaster; others decidedly sit below deck on a large institutional vessel trying not to make waves; and still more identify as a marionette, being pulled in many directions by those in higher positions. Indeed, the unique and important role of middle manager conjures these images and more.

Although middle managers deal with much conflict in their role, there are many positive aspects of the position. Middle managers should identify the place they hold in their institutions and avail themselves of the opportunities for professional and personal growth that often accompany this time in a career. For many middle managers, this is a prime opportunity to become a mentor to entry-level professionals and enhance supervisory skills. Some middle managers take advantage of the prospect of obtaining a terminal degree or starting a family during this time. Before experiencing the pressures that come with holding a senior management position, middle managers should utilize the time in their positions to prepare for their next career opportunity. If ever there was a training ground for student affairs professionals, middle management is an excellent place for leaders to sharpen a skill set, gain new expertise, make mistakes, and thoughtfully explore the career opportunities that exist.

To assist this process, senior management must set clear expectations for middle managers, offer training programs, and establish mechanisms for ongoing communication and feedback. A simple orientation for mid-level managers is not adequate for the challenges and conflict that they face; ongoing support is crucial. With these important mechanisms in place, when the inevitable conflicts arise, middle managers are likely to possess the suitable framework to manage each situation appropriately and more comfortably.

Although managing conflict can be uncomfortable, it is also an opportunity to identify areas for institutional growth. Successfully mediating conflict can also boost middle managers' confidence, thereby making them more effective as leaders in student affairs. Providing middle managers with the appropriate training opportunities, resources, and support will allow them to function at a higher level professionally for the betterment of students, staff, and the institution.

Managing conflict is a vital skill for middle managers, as well as others in student affairs. Middle managers can be positive role models throughout an institution, especially for new professionals and graduate students. The next chapter discusses how middle managers can successfully supervise graduate students.

References

ACPA/NASPA. Professional Competency Areas for Student Affairs Practicioners: Informing Intentional Professional Development Design and Selection, Working Draft. Washington, D.C.: ACPA/NASPA, 2010.

American Council on Higher Education. *The Student Personnel Point of View.* Washington, D.C.: NASPA, 1949.

Clegg, S., and McAuley, J. "Conceptualising Middle Management in Higher Education: A Multifaceted Discourse." *Journal of Higher Education Policy and Management*, 2005, 27(1), 19–34.

Dunnette, M. D., Kraut, A. I., Pedigo, P. R., and McKenna, D. D. "The Role of the Manager: What's Really Important in Different Management Jobs." *Academy of Management Executive*, 2005, 19(4), 122–129.

Frunzi, G., and Halloran, J. *Supervision: The Art of Management.* Englewood Cliffs, N.J.: Prentice Hall, 1991.

Gajda, A. *The Trials of Academe: The New Era of Campus Litigation.* Cambridge: Harvard University Press, 2009.

Mather, P. C., Bryan, S. P., and Faulkner, W. O. "Orienting Mid-Level Student Affairs Professionals." *College Student Affairs Journal*, 2009, 27(2), 242–256.

Mills, D. B. "The Role of the Middle Manager." In M. J. Barr, M. K. Desler, and Associates (eds.), *The Handbook of Student Affairs Administration.* San Francisco: Jossey-Bass, 2000.

Scott, J. E. "Creating Effective Staff Management Programs." In M. J. Barr, M. K. Desler, & Associates (eds.), *The Handbook of Student Affairs Administration*. San Francisco: Jossey-Bass, 2000.

MARY-BETH COOPER is senior vice president for student affairs at Rochester Institute of Technology.

HEATH BOICE-PARDEE is associate vice president for student affairs at Rochester Institute of Technology.

New Directions for Student Services • DOI: 10.1002/ss

This chapter describes the nuances, challenges, and rewards of supervising graduate assistants in student affairs master's programs.

Supervising Graduate Assistants

Jessica White, John Nonnamaker

Discussions of personnel management in student affairs literature and at national conferences often focus on supervising new or midlevel professionals and the myriad challenges and possibilities these relationships entail (Carpenter, 2001; Winston and Creamer, 1997). Graduate students as employees and the often-complicated and ill-structured supervisory relationships that exist for them are frequently overlooked or mentioned only briefly in such leadership conversations (Dalton, 2003; Kouzes and Posner, 2003). This oversight is not unique to discussions of graduate student supervision, though, as the graduate student experience is generally underrepresented in scholarly literature (Bair, Haworth, and Sandfort, 2004; Guentzel and Nesheim, 2006).

The purpose of this chapter is to call attention to the graduate student as an employee and consider the complex relationships that can exist between supervisors and graduate assistants. In this chapter the authors provide a brief overview of graduate students on university campuses; offer an introduction to the traditional roles and functions of graduate assistants; discuss the complexity, challenges, and opportunities that supervisors face in working with graduate assistants in student affairs settings; and review implications and offer suggestions.

Historical and Demographic Overview of Graduate Students

For many years, graduate students have held leadership or mentorship roles on university and college campuses, with responsibilities to provide service to and educate younger generations of scholars. Historically, the graduate student's role was that of an advanced learner or tutor under the

New Directions for Student Services, no. 136, Winter 2011 © Wiley Periodicals, Inc.
Published online in Wiley Online Library (wileyonlinelibrary.com) • DOI: 10.1002/ss.413

tutelage of a specific faculty member, but as institutional enrollments increased, their function changed to include faculty-in-training and administrator-in-training duties as well (Lucas, 2006).

While graduate degrees were awarded as early as the mid-1850s, graduate degree attainment did not swell until after World War II as returning veterans took advantage of the Serviceman's Readjustment Act (also known as the GI Bill) in droves (Lucas, 2006). During the 1949–1950 academic year, postsecondary enrollments rose to nearly half a million, a substantial increase from just 50 years earlier when approximately 29,000 undergraduate degrees were awarded (Lucas, 2006). To respond to these rapidly increasing enrollments, universities tapped graduate students to help meet the growing demand for instruction and service. As a result, in the years following World War II, graduate education grew even faster than undergraduate enrollments; the number of PhDs doubled every eleven years (Lucas, 2006).

Growth in graduate enrollment in the United States has been relatively consistent over the past ten years, with a 3.7 percent annual increase (Bell, 2010). According to the Council of Graduate Schools' most recent data (Bell, 2010), total graduate enrollment increased 4.7 percent between fall 2008 and fall 2009. In the fall of 2009, nearly 1.8 million students enrolled in graduate programs. More than half of these students were enrolled in programs in education, business, and health sciences. Of these 1.8 million students, more than 463,000 enrolled for the first time in a certificate, education specialist, master's, or doctoral program. Much of the growth in total graduate enrollment has been the result of considerable increases in the number of international students/temporary residents, women, and U.S. racial/ethnic minorities. Over the past decade, enrollment of temporary residents and women has increased 4.2 percent and 5.2 percent, respectively, on average annually. Total enrollment for U.S. racial/ethnic minorities has increased at a faster rate than that of Whites in nearly every broad field over the past ten years.

According to a report prepared by the U.S. Department of Education's National Center for Education Statistics (2009), 328,979 graduate students, or nearly 10 percent of all institutional personnel, were employed in assistantship positions at degree-granting institutions nationally in 2007. This figure represents an increase of 47.7 percent over the two decades spanning 1987 to 2007 and was a greater percentage gain than both executive/administrative/managerial staff and faculty. Given the prevalence and continued rapid growth of graduate students employed at universities, it is important to consider how their circumstances may be unique in relation to supervision.

Roles and Functions of Graduate Assistants

Supervised assistantship appointments on campuses differ by discipline and unit, but nearly always provide valuable opportunities to gain experi-

NEW DIRECTIONS FOR STUDENT SERVICES • DOI: 10.1002/ss

ence and to pay the expenses of graduate study. As noted by Ethington and Pisani (1993), graduate assistantships (GAs) provide "an opportunity for socialization into the academic profession" (p. 344) via an apprenticeship-like experience. Additionally, the responsibilities associated with the graduate assistantship help to promote institutional, disciplinary, and departmental community and assist graduate students with professional identity (Lovitts and Nelson, 2000; White and Nonnamaker, 2008). In this way, the GA position plays an important role in the graduate students' social and academic integration, constructs that Vincent Tinto (1993) identified as pivotal in students' decisions to depart from or remain at the institution (Girves and Wemmerus, 1988; Golde, 2000; Lovitts and Nelson, 2000).

Graduate assistantship experiences generally fall into one of two categories: graduate research assistantships (GRAs) or graduate teaching assistantships (GTAs) (Ethington and Pisani, 1993). Graduate research assistantships are prevalent at research-intensive institutions, as graduate students are employed to assist with funded research projects directed by faculty members. Graduate research assistants' duties often include conducting library searches, developing laboratory protocols, and completing data entry and analyses. In comparison, graduate teaching assistants have responsibilities to instruct undergraduate classes, including lab and discussion sections, with duties ranging from developing the overall course curriculum to delivering lectures and grading student assignments. For the purposes of this chapter and discussion, the authors will use the more general umbrella term of *graduate assistantship* (GA), acknowledging that this may include research, teaching, or more administrative responsibilities.

Within many student affairs master's programs, GA positions with a service component have become increasingly common, supplementing or replacing the more familiar research and teaching duties. For example, it is not unusual for graduate students in student affairs master's programs to be employed as graduate teaching assistants, resident directors, academic advisors, conduct officers, recreational sports coordinators, or campus activities programmers. Such positions are often closely aligned with students' professional goals and provide valuable service to the college or university, but are not officially located within or supervised by the academic program. So, while the impact of these graduate assistant positions is far reaching for both the student and institution, supervising students in such varied experiences that in many cases are beyond the academic department or college can be challenging. As noted earlier, literature regarding graduate student supervision is lacking. Yet the unique experiences of graduate assistants in student affairs master's programs warrant purposeful consideration and discussion. In the following sections, the authors use their varied experiences as student affairs professionals, faculty, and graduate assistant supervisors to inform their ideas and address key challenges and opportunities with respect to supervising graduate assistants.

NEW DIRECTIONS FOR STUDENT SERVICES • DOI: 10.1002/ss

Challenges and Opportunities in Supervising Graduate Assistants

Those supervising graduate assistants in student affairs master's programs might find the process and overall experience different from the more common practice of supervising professional or administrative staff or even undergraduate student workers. Some of the more common challenges associated with supervising graduate assistants include: (1) role conflict, (2) persistence to degree completion and graduate student turnover, and (3) disconnection between assistantship area and the student's academic program. Each of these challenges along with potential opportunities will be discussed here in greater detail.

Role Conflict. Supervising graduate assistants in student affairs master's programs often requires the supervisor to assume multiple roles such as manager, mentor, teacher, and advisor. While at times related and intersecting, these varied roles can also compete with one another and create tension for the supervisor and the graduate assistant who is at once an employee, student affairs professional-in-training, and student. Depending on the relationship between the graduate student and the supervisor, these roles may be straightforward and clearly understood, complementary, or overlapping, or may be ill defined and come into conflict with each other. Role conflict results when the supervisor assumes two or more different and potentially incompatible roles concurrently. The ability to seamlessly navigate between and among supervisory roles can prove problematic at times, but offers potential for dialogue and growth.

The manager role is characterized by providing instruction and evaluation as well as being responsible for the work and productivity of the employee. Compensation, feedback, and accountability are key features in a managerial relationship. The role with respect to this function is relatively straightforward and is likely familiar to the supervisor and graduate assistant.

Given that the graduate assistant is a student affairs professional-in-training, the supervisor may also serve as a mentor. According to Bozeman and Feeney (2007):

> Mentoring is a process for the informal transmission of knowledge, social capital, and the psychosocial support perceived by the recipient as relevant to work, career, or professional development; mentoring entails informal communication, usually face-to-face and during a sustained period of time, between a person who is perceived to have greater relevant knowledge, wisdom, or experience (the mentor) and a person who is perceived to have less (the protégé). (p. 731)

Within a student affairs setting, supervisors may also be mentors in that they are assisting students in applying what they are learning in the

New Directions for Student Services • DOI: 10.1002/ss

classroom to their jobs. The supervisor as mentor takes on the responsibility to socialize new student affairs professionals to the field, including current issues, professional ethics, and networking opportunities.

In the teacher role, the supervisor may simultaneously serve as an in-class instructor for the student affairs master's student. Given the strong emphasis on practice and application, many student affairs master's programs rely heavily on the expertise of working professionals at their institutions to teach for-credit graduate courses. Instruction, feedback, and accountability are foundational in a teaching relationship, where the instructor is responsible for assessing the degree to which standards and learning outcomes have been achieved.

Similar to the role of mentor, the advisor serves as someone with greater knowledge in a particular field who imparts that knowledge to someone with less knowledge. This can happen as an academic advisor who ultimately approves a student's program of study or thesis work or as someone who makes suggestions regarding course selection or internship experiences. As with the teacher role, it is not uncommon for student affairs administrators to employ graduate assistants while also formally advising graduate students toward completing their degrees.

These varied and intersecting roles of manager, mentor, teacher, and advisor can be incompatible at times, creating tension for the supervisor and the graduate assistant. For example, if the supervisor is serving in a traditional managerial role as well as academic advisor or instructor within the student affairs graduate program, the supervisor is challenged with evaluating the graduate student as an employee and student simultaneously. The graduate student may excel in one area and struggle in another. Is the supervisor able to separate the student's performance in these two different contexts? Is the student able to differentiate between the individual as his supervisor and his advisor or instructor?

Similarly, those supervising graduate assistants often are challenged to balance the roles of manager and mentor. While graduate assistants are considered employees of the university, assistantship positions are in many ways apprenticeships, opportunities for graduate students to become acquainted with academic culture. In the case of student affairs graduate students, assistantships provide valuable "in-the-field" and hands-on work experience, often under the tutelage of experienced student affairs practitioners. In this respect, supervisors can find themselves juggling day-to-day management with the broader responsibilities of mentorship. Certainly, supervision and mentorship are not mutually exclusive, but in supervising the student affairs graduate student, the roles may become blurred if the student desires more professional grooming and networking and less evaluation or accountability. This might be a problem for the supervisor to serve as a reference or assist with networking opportunities. Which role provides the context for the type and amount of information that is shared? Similarly, the supervisor may view mentorship as beyond the scope of his or her responsibilities, creating tension with the graduate assistant, who views the assistantship as primarily a venue for professional development and networking. In this case, is the supervisor required or expected to serve as a mentor, formally or informally? Does the supervisor have the desire or skills to even do so?

Complicating the nature of these relationships further is how the student is funded and by whom. Differences in the source of funding may confuse roles as to who exactly is "in charge" and to whom the student should report. For example, is the funding via the academic department, from a unit within student affairs, or linked directly to a research grant received by a faculty member? Graduate assistants might find themselves torn between program faculty and a student affairs assistantship supervisor if the faculty and supervisor provide conflicting professional advice or have different priorities for the student's time. This can be particularly challenging when academic and administrative deadlines collide.

Despite the challenges, the role conflict experienced by supervisors overseeing graduate students may present opportunities for stronger working relationships with graduate assistants. In circumstances where the supervisor is also the instructor or academic advisor, unique possibilities exist for the supervisor to get to know the graduate student in a variety of contexts and over the course of several years. Within the context of these multiple roles, lifelong collegial relationships can be formed. Role conflict can be an invitation for the supervisor to initiate an intentional conversation with the graduate assistant regarding roles and boundaries. This not only assists the student in the short term, but also models professional behavior for when the student becomes a supervisor.

Persistence to Degree Completion and Graduate Student Turnover. Persistence to degree completion is not a new area of research, but the topic as it relates to graduate students has gained recent national attention given the economy, increasing student debt, and dwindling institutional resources (Berger, 2007; Glenn, 2006; Smallwood, 2004). These authors have called attention to the relatively low ten-year completion rate of doctoral students, a figure that differs by discipline from 47 percent (humanities) to 64 percent (engineering) (Denecke, 2005). Researchers have examined reasons for this alarmingly low statistic, including inadequate financial resources, poor relations between students and faculty, dissatisfaction with graduate program, inability to remain motivated and work independently, and difficulty in establishing a sense of community (Golde, 2000, 2005; Kerlin, 1995; Lovitts and Nelson, 2000; Sowell and Zhang, 2007; White and Nonnamaker, 2008). Independent of the reasons, these relatively low completion rates coupled with shorter degree programs (one to two years in many cases among student affairs master's programs) and graduate students' tendency to "stop-out" at various points during their educational journey point to the stark reality that universities experience high turnover in their graduate student population.

Graduate student turnover can occur for other reasons than persistence to degree completion and may result in the student's leaving the graduate assistantship but not the degree program. A recent phenomenon in higher education discussed at professional conferences but yet to appear in the literature suggests that graduate assistants are being hired for various roles in response to budget cuts instead of as full-time or part-time staff. These graduate assistants are expected to maintain similar workload expectations as professional staff. These expectations can lead to graduate assistants' feeling overwhelmed and wanting to leave the position, if not the degree program.

For the graduate assistant supervisor, turnover can pose significant challenges. Hiring and training any new employee is an investment on the part of the organization. As such, having to rehire, provide orientation to, and retrain an employee every year or two can be disruptive to the department or unit and can pose a burden on time and resources.

Graduate assistants are no exception to this, and the frequency of their turnover as a result of varied academic reasons may be felt more immediately as their duties within student affairs settings are often "front-line" with responsibilities critical to the day-to-day functioning of a unit. For example, training and developing a graduate assistant to perform in the role of a resident director or academic advisor can require skills and knowledge specific to that campus or unit. Learning about policies, procedures, and campus resources can take many months of on-the-job experience. If the graduate assistant moves on to other employment opportunities at the end of the academic year, the supervisor may be faced with the challenge of identifying, hiring, and retraining a new graduate assistant. The repetition of this cycle can lead to the potential disruption of essential duties, as it can take considerable time to get a new employee trained and effectively contributing to the unit. Also, given the nature of academic calendars, the student might not be available to work during the summer months. All of these can compromise organizational continuity and sustainability of service.

The frequent turnover of graduate assistants may take its toll on an organization in additional ways. Graduate assistants' relatively short tenure in their positions can significantly hinder the establishment of key working relationships. Knowing or assuming that graduate assistants will be employees for only a year or two, full-time employees who must work closely with graduate assistants may be reluctant to rely on graduate assistants for long-term projects or planning and may prefer to limit graduate assistant responsibilities. This can be particularly challenging in units such as new-student programs and orientation, campus activities, and residence life, which require continuous planning for the next academic cycle. Similarly, in positions where establishing and maintaining strong relationships with students is essential to doing quality work, graduate assistant turnover can be problematic. For example, in areas like academic advising, health

NEW DIRECTIONS FOR STUDENT SERVICES • DOI: 10.1002/ss

services, and career counseling, where ongoing and consistent interaction with students often results in better service, a new graduate assistant employee every year may alienate students who have come to know and rely on a key individual for support and may have an impact on the continuity of learning.

The frequency of graduate assistant turnover is not without its opportunities. While at times the change in personnel can be a distraction, a new employee in any organization has the potential to be energizing. Graduate assistants have the unique advantage of being both a student and an employee, a position that can afford them a rich perspective, especially when they share generational traits with current undergraduates, which may inform program and service delivery. As a result, graduate assistants might have deeper knowledge of student cultures and needs and have fresher ideas than older full-time staff members. Graduate students in student affairs programs who are directly working in the field have current research and theory from which to draw. In turn, these graduate assistants can "teach" or share this information with others in the organization who do not have a formal educational background in student affairs or whose degrees were obtained a number of years prior. In this way, new graduate students may have a rejuvenating effect on the organization.

Disconnection Between Assistantship Area and Academic Program. A third potential challenge in supervising graduate assistants in student affairs master's programs is the potential disconnection between the assistantship area and the formal academic program. This can occur when graduate assistants are employed beyond the student affairs master's program in diverse campus offices such as residence life, career services, or Greek life in other academic units doing academic advising, orientation, or other college-specific duties. The application of classroom learning to a professional practitioner setting is an essential component of most student affairs graduate programs. Graduate students in these programs are expected to integrate in-class learning into everyday practice. Assistantship positions often serve as the primary setting for student affairs graduate students to test new knowledge and skills. As such, the assistantship supervisor can play a critical role by supporting integration of in-class and out-of-class experiences or discouraging these efforts.

Supporting or discouraging the integration of graduate students' classroom learning and assistantship tasks may occur for a variety of reasons. Assistantship supervisors who also serve as faculty members or advisors in the graduate program are likely to be familiar with the learning goals and outcomes of the academic program and support the educational efforts of the program. For graduate assistants in these areas, the integration of learning and practice may be rather seamless.

However, for supervisors on campus who are not part of the student affairs academic program, assisting with the integration of graduate assistants' in-class learning and out-of-class practice may be challenging. For example, a graduate assistant may be employed as an academic advisor for science or engineering students and have a supervisor who has little or no knowledge of the student affairs graduate program or profession. Thus, the supervisor's ability to provide feedback or direction related to student affairs–specific topics can be limited.

In other circumstances, supervisors, especially those not closely affiliated with the students affairs degree program, may be hesitant for graduate students to use their assistantship positions as training grounds for new ideas and practice. Supervisors might be concerned that this type of experimentation will lead to errors or, at the very least, a reduction in efficiency. Contrasted with this, many graduate assistants in student affairs master's programs expect to integrate academic experiences with their assistantship responsibilities and are dissatisfied if those opportunities are not present. In some cases, the supervisors seek to learn about the graduate program to support the graduate assistant's expectations or renegotiate the nature of the assistantship position so that the graduate assistant has specific duties that are appropriate for integrating classroom learning with professional experience. In other circumstances, though, the supervisor may choose to maintain current practice and limit the graduate assistant's opportunities to apply in-class learning within the assistantship position. This in turn may lead to additional graduate assistant turnover, as the graduate assistant may seek other employment at the institution that meets this goal.

The disconnection between the assistantship area and the academic program can also be attributed at times to the graduate assistant. As assistantship positions often include tuition remission or waivers for the graduate student, graduate assistant positions are usually in high demand. And while graduate assistant positions with student affairs master's programs typically span numerous administrative units, there are often positions or functional areas that are more desirable among graduate students. As a result, some graduate students in student affairs master's programs accept positions that do not directly align with their professional interests and goals. For the graduate assistant, this might equate to a lack of investment in the unit, a disconnection between the academic program and the assistantship experience, with the graduate assistant purposefully seeking to integrate classroom learning in other functional areas more closely related to his or her career aspirations.

Assistantship supervisors and the staff in their offices who embrace the presence of graduate students in a student affairs program can benefit from integrating student development theory and other elements of the graduate assistant's academic experiences into their services and practices. Improvements in areas such as assessment and student engagement might result, and staff may gain an increased appreciation for the diversity of student populations on their campus. In this way, these graduate students also serve as an important bridge between the formal learning within academic departments and the current practice within student affairs divisions.

NEW DIRECTIONS FOR STUDENT SERVICES • DOI: 10.1002/ss

Implications and Recommendations for Practice

Role conflict can occur when one is forced to assume two different and potentially incompatible roles. Supervisors can, however, minimize the role conflicts or their impact in three ways: (1) encourage the graduate student to develop multiple mentoring relationships, (2) support the department in establishing clear and transparent roles, expectations, and responsibilities, and (3) implement departmental policies and procedures to minimize and mitigate role conflicts. Encouraging graduate students to develop multiple mentors provides the student with various professional role models whose styles might align more closely with that of the student or whose backgrounds might socialize the student into the culture of student affairs or a particular functional area. In addition, multiple mentors can assist students in achieving their academic and professional goals.

Establishing clear and transparent goals, personal and professional boundaries, responsibilities, and expectations may also assist in avoiding role conflict. One example of good practice is implementing and widely distributing departmental guidelines that articulate roles, expectations, benchmarks, timelines of success, and milestones. Learning agreements or compacts can provide additional structure to ensure that the graduate assistant is clear as to the role and duties of the supervisor. Annual formal reviews of student progress could also be used as a way to address ongoing misconceptions the graduate assistant may have and to clarify supervisor and student roles. Finally, departments should also develop clear procedures to follow, including either a departmentally or institutionally based ombudsperson if role conflicts do emerge.

In responding to issues of graduate assistant turnover, supervisors would do well first to recognize that graduate assistant employment is more fluid, that the hiring and training cycle is repeated more frequently than with full-time employees. As a result, supervisors of graduate assistants should look to develop well-organized hiring and training practices to ensure that the transition of new graduate assistants is as streamlined and efficient as possible. Involving several people from the unit in training of graduate assistants may be beneficial to ensure consistency from year to year. As part of the hiring process, graduate assistant supervisors may also want to create graduate assistant positions that have flexible or shared duties. Doing so might allow graduate assistants to form partnerships with more experienced personnel, and might also mitigate the impact of turnover.

Supervisors may want to consider additional training or support for department personnel who work with new graduate assistants each year and have to frequently adapt to and rely on new colleagues. Reframing the perception that the somewhat transient nature of graduate assistants is an opportunity rather than a shortcoming can go a long way in terms of maintaining positive staff dynamics.

NEW DIRECTIONS FOR STUDENT SERVICES • DOI: 10.1002/ss

As disconnection between the assistantship area and the graduate assistant's academic program may pose considerable challenges, supervisors of graduate assistants may want to develop partnerships with student affairs academic programs to be well informed regarding students' in-class experiences and outcomes. In some cases, these partnerships exist in regular faculty–assistantship supervisor meetings, exchange of course syllabi, invitations for supervisors to attend classes, and email listservs. Making the most of these opportunities can help bridge the potential gap that can often exist between formal and informal learning. Also, graduate assistant supervisors may address the potential disconnection between classroom learning and assistantship practice by inviting graduate assistants to share their learning with others. Staff meetings, in-service sessions, or informal conversations may provide fertile ground for the graduate assistants to make connections and for the staff to learn as well. In cases where the integration between the academic program and the assistantship is problematic, not appropriate, or not desired by the student, the supervisor must be clear with the graduate assistant about these expectations. While the assistantship may not be the means by which graduate assistants test their classroom learning, the supervisor may want to be prepared to offer suggestions about ways in which the graduate assistant may get the needed theory-to-practice experience, such as internship or volunteer opportunities.

Conclusion

Given the number of graduate assistants within student affairs master's programs, it is important to consider ways in which graduate assistants are supervised. And while numerous challenges exist, the supervisor–graduate assistant relationship is rife with opportunities for personal, professional, and institutional growth. Effective graduate assistant supervision is an essential component in cultivating the next generation of university administrators and faculty. Effective supervision of graduate assistants benefits the student, the supervisor, the institution, and the overall profession.

In the next chapter, Tricia Scarcia-King discusses virtual supervision, an emerging area of responsibility in higher education, but a topic similar to supervising graduate students in that it has received little attention in the literature of supervision.

References

Bair, C. R., Haworth, J. G., and Sandfort, M. "Doctoral Student Learning and Development: A Shared Responsibility." *NASPA Journal*, 2004, 709–727.

Bell, N. E. "Graduate Enrollment and Degrees: 1999 to 2009." Washington, D.C.: Council of Graduate Schools, 2010.

Berger, J. "Exploring Ways to Shorten the Ascent to a Ph.D." *New York Times*, October 4, 2007, B3.

Bozeman, B., and Feeney, M. "Toward a Useful Theory of Mentoring: A Conceptual Analysis and Critique. *Administration and Society*, 2007, 39(6), 719–739.

Carpenter, D. S. "Staffing Student Affairs Divisions." In R. B. Winston Jr., D. G. Creamer, T. K. Miller, and Associates (eds.), *The Professional Student Affairs Administrator: Educator, Leader, and Manager* (pp. 211–243). New York: Brunner-Routledge, 2001.

Dalton, J. C. "Managing Human Resources." In S. R. Komives, D. B. Woodard Jr., and Associates (eds.), *Student Services: A Handbook for the Profession* (4th ed., pp. 397–422). San Francisco: Jossey-Bass, 2003.

Denecke, D. D. "Ph.D. Completion Project: Preliminary Results from Baseline Data." *CGS Communicator*, 2005, 38, 1–4.

Ethington, C. A., and Pisani, A. "The RA and TA Experience: Impediments and Benefits to Graduate Study." *Research in Higher Education*, 1993, 34, 343–354.

Girves, J. E., and Wemmerus, V. "Developing Models of Graduate Student Degree Progress." *Journal of Higher Education*, 1988, 59(2), 163–189.

Glenn, D. "Economists Ponder How to Speed Up Ph.D. Completion." *Chronicle of Higher Education*, January 20, 2006, A24.

Golde, C. M. "Should I Stay or Should I Go? Student Descriptions of the Doctoral Attrition Process." *Review of Higher Education*, 2000, 23, 199–227.

Golde, C. M. "The Role of the Department and Discipline in Doctoral Student Attrition: Lessons from Four Departments." *Journal of Higher Education*, 2005, 76, 669–700.

Guentzel, M. J., and Nesheim, B. E. *Supporting Graduate and Professional Students: The Role of Student Affairs.* New Directions for Student Services, no. 115. San Francisco: Jossey-Bass, 2006.

Kerlin, S. P. "Pursuit of the Ph.D.: 'Survival of the Fittest' or is it Time for a New Approach?" *Education Policy Analysis*, 3, 16, 1995. Retrieved January 29, 2007, from http://epaa.asu.edu/epaa/v3n16.html.

Kouzes, J. M., and Posner, B. Z. *The Jossey-Bass Academic Administrator's Guide to Exemplary Leadership.* San Francisco: Jossey-Bass, 2003.

Lovitts, B. E., and Nelson, C. "The Hidden Crisis in Graduate Education: Attrition from Ph.D. Programs." *Academe,* 2000, 86(6), 44–50.

Lucas, C. J. *American Higher Education: A History* (2nd ed.). New York: Palgrave Macmillan, 2006.

Smallwood, S. "Doctor Dropout." *Chronicle of Higher Education,* January 16, 2004, B4.

Sowell, R., and Zhang, T. "Completion and Attrition: Program Baseline Data." Paper presented at the annual meeting of The Council of Graduate Schools, Seattle, Dec. 4, 2007.

Tinto, V. *Leaving College* (2nd ed.). Chicago: University of Chicago Press, 1993.

U.S. Department of Education Institute of Education Sciences, National Center for Education Statistics. *Digest of Education Statistics: 2009.* Retrieved January 29, 2010, from http://nces.ed.gov/programs/digest/d09/index.asp.

White, J., and Nonnamaker, J. "Belonging and Mattering: How Science Doctoral Students Experience Community." *NASPA Journal*, 2008, 45, 350–372.

Winston, Jr., R. B., and Creamer, D. G. *Improving Staffing Practices in Student Affairs.* San Francisco: Jossey-Bass, 1997.

JESSICA WHITE, PHD, *is an assistant professor in adult education and higher education leadership in the College of Education at Oregon State University.*

JOHN NONNAMAKER, PHD, *is executive director of the Office of Career Services at Providence College.*

6

This chapter provides an analysis of the virtual workplace, including the dynamics of supervision across time and distance, and provides effective strategies to enhance your supervisory portfolio.

Effective Strategies for Virtual Supervision

Trisha J. Scarcia-King

Anyone who's seen the 1960s cartoon *The Jetsons* has insight into the challenges of virtual supervision. *The Jetsons* serves as an interesting reflection on the role of technology in the workplace. The animated cartoon was based on science fiction and projected to take place during the twenty-first century, circa 2062 (see http://www.tv.com/the-jetsons/show/3723 /summary.html). The cartoon's main character, George Jetson, commuted to work in a compact aero car that transported him through the sky. George often communicated with his quick-tempered boss, Mr. Spacely, via a big screen, which he accessed with the press of a button. Thus, the Jetsons lived in a high-technology environment, one that was more advanced than the technology actually available in society at the time.

The use of technology in student affairs is not as advanced as depicted in *The Jetsons*. However, there has been a steady increase in the use of technology to enhance the education, programs, services, and support of the students on our campuses. Technology changes rapidly, and the use of it differs with comfort, interest, access, and adaptability to technological advancements.

This chapter explores virtual supervision and its application to student affairs. I consider three tenets of student affairs supervision—relationships, teamwork, and achieving mission effectiveness—and address the roles required of those responsible for virtual supervision.

Higher Education's Landscape

The landscape of higher education provides a basis for understanding the variations in student affairs practices. Land-grant universities, multicampus

NEW DIRECTIONS FOR STUDENT SERVICES, no. 136, Winter 2011 © Wiley Periodicals, Inc.
Published online in Wiley Online Library (wileyonlinelibrary.com) • DOI: 10.1002/ss.414

systems with two-year or four-year degree programs, and private vocational and liberal arts schools provide different formats for course delivery, support services, and cocurricular engagement. The methods include in-person and synchronous or asynchronous online or a combination of each. The number of online classes has increased significantly at both traditional, land-based institutions and those serving students primarily via online instruction. In their *Learning on Demand* report, Allen and Seaman (2010) noted an increase of three million students, over six years, taking one or more online courses. In addition, they indicated that the outlook suggests "no immediate leveling off" (Allen and Seaman, 2010, p. 5). Therefore, further growth in online instruction is expected.

Communication from universities to registered students is now beyond standard business letters mailed to permanent addresses. Many institutions offer electronic platforms for a host of support services, such as admissions, financial aid applications, course registration, emergency notifications, and housing assignments, among others. Electronic platforms, such as Org Sync, have been developed for student engagement in clubs and organizations. Further, a host of social media programs, such as Facebook and Twitter, offer free membership to engage in conversation and information exchange on the World Wide Web. These programs can be linked to cell phones and institutional Web sites to enhance information sharing among members and from the institution to others in the campus, local, and regional communities and nationwide.

Growth in the use of electronic platforms for course instruction, support services, and student affairs programs requires supervisors to adapt to the changing technology landscape and expand their skills so that they can effectively supervise in settings with very limited face-to-face interaction, mixed environments (those that involve face-to-face and virtual interaction), or technology alone.

Virtual Supervision

In a virtual setting, challenges of time and distance can be a barrier to communication and result in diminished effectiveness. Some supervisors have trouble managing employees in face-to-face settings. Imagine yourself in a situation where you have the added dynamic of distance or virtual space separating the employee and supervisor. How is this relationship managed? How can a supervisor effectively balance the responsibility of meeting the institution's needs and those of the employee in a virtual setting? How does the supervisor attend to the learning and growth needs of the employee? How does a supervisor go about influencing the employee's performance? These dynamics of virtual supervision may best be illuminated with examples from student affairs and comparisons to other business environments. Implications and recommended strategies to address these challenges are provided later in our discussion.

New Directions for Student Services • DOI: 10.1002/ss

If you are a digital native, techniques to enhance virtual supervision may be more natural for you (Presnsky, 2001). Digital immigrants, those individuals who did not grow up with technology as an aspect of their daily lives, may face more challenges in adapting to virtual supervision (Presnsky, 2001). There has been little research on the concept of virtual supervision or its application to the field of student affairs. Yet, the responsibility to supervise in a virtual environment has been thrust upon some student affairs professionals.

Tenets of Supervision in Student Affairs

In many respects, the role of Mr. Spacely, George Jetson's boss, was a reflection of the 1960s style of centralized decision making (Robbins and Judge, 2007). Mr. Spacely made all the decisions. Supervisors in this paradigm, ". . . lead by administrative fiat. They gave orders, issued edicts and made rules" (Ramsey, 1989, p. 2). Purely centralized decision making reflects business values that are not compatible with contemporary methods for effective virtual supervision in student affairs. Supervision in student affairs requires flexible skills that can be readily applied to organizations that are centralized or decentralized, or have networks where information flows freely in all directions (Robbins and Judge, 2007).

Student support services and student affairs divisions are distinct from one institution to the next, as are the expectations of supervisors. However, there are three generally accepted tenets of supervision in student affairs: the importance of relationships, the value of teamwork, and the importance of achieving mission effectiveness. In addition, attending to the professional development of staff is an important component of a supervisor's role. I will explore how supervising in mixed or virtual environments might influence relationships, teamwork, and mission effectiveness.

Importance of Relationships. Supervisors have a unique responsibility for the tenor of the work relationship with the employees who report to them. Roper (2002, p. 14), in describing the importance of professional relationships, said, "There is no such thing as an unimportant or insignificant relationship." Because the relationships between a supervisor and his or her direct reports are important to the success of the individual and organization, the supervisor should be quite intentional about efforts to develop and sustain those relationships.

DuPree's (1989) five steps for developing healthy relationships within the work environment include: (1) respect people and believe in the diversity of what individuals contribute; (2) understand that what we believe precedes policy and practice; (3) agree on the rights of work; (4) understand the respective role and relationship of contractual agreements and covenants; and (5) understand that relationships count more than structure. This focus on relationships emphasizes a belief in the significance of the individual employee and is foundational to providing employees an opportunity to construct their work environment and contribute to the institutional goals. When virtual supervisors acknowledge that the most essential role they have is to create a positive work relationship with their supervisees, they will be well on the way to creating an environment in which employees can successfully carry out their job responsibilities.

Roper (2002, p. 13) provides both a succinct definition and a method for developing effective relationships. He begins by contending that relationships can be viewed as a series of conversations, and "in order to construct a positive relationship it is imperative that we create a history of successful conversations." Roper's notion of "successful conversations," combined with DuPree's (1989) recognition of the centrality of supervisees in the relationship, suggests an ongoing process that strives toward the goal of mutual understanding and positive interaction between the supervisor and supervisee.

In face-to-face settings, successful conversations may take place in one-on-one meetings with individuals or in groups such as departmental or division meetings. Mixed or virtual settings, however, present barriers of time, distance, and location; thus, the methods for achieving effective relationships differ in those settings.

Because of the important role of nonverbal communication, supervisors and supervisees should pay attention to the nuance or tone of communication conducted by email, instant message, text, phone, or Web conference. Because of the potential for misunderstanding or misinterpretation, those communicating in virtual contexts may need to be even more attentive to the subtleties of communication than in face-to-face settings (Robbins and Judge, 2007, p. 374). To promote successful virtual relationships, supervisors should develop avenues to build stronger relationships and communication with employees. Examples of these avenues include allowing sufficient time at the beginning of meetings for informal discussions and interpersonal exchanges; taking time to recognize birthdays or personal achievements; building time into conversations to acknowledge and appreciate the employee; and allowing for time at the end of meetings to clarify next steps or what the supervisee may need from the supervisor to carry out responsibilities. A small effort to recognize individuals can strengthen connections and create ease within communications later. If guided by a sincere and intentional effort, the work relationship will grow positively. Having strong relationships with supervisees provides a firm foundation for daily interaction and makes it easier for the supervisee to understand the supervisor's needs and expectations.

Value of Teamwork. The second tenet for effective supervision in student affairs is constructing a team environment. For the sake of this discussion, a *team* is defined as a group of individuals working together to achieve shared goals. Dominant characteristics of a team are information sharing, joint decision making, continuous learning, collaboration, and continuous improvement (Zenger, Musselwhite, Hurson, and Perrin,

1994). Virtual supervisors can create a team environment by giving attention to how they can influence the achievement of the preceding components in their communication and action planning.

An important attribute of a good team member is the ability to understand the significance of a project and see it through to completion, regardless of the level of ease or enjoyment involved in the process (Auer Jones, 2010). Individuals on a team must demonstrate collegiality and willingness to contribute to others' projects. In a virtual environment, this is demonstrated through timeliness, consistency of completed tasks, and feedback. The virtual supervisor or message sender can streamline responses to a specific virtual folder that can be created for the messages as a way of cataloging the history of communication within a team and among individuals.

Roper suggests that important behaviors in a team environment include maintaining perspective and staying humble (2002, p. 98). This involves learning to set one's personal needs, pride, or ego aside to serve the department, division, and institutional mission. The ability to be group-centered is an indication of willingness to be a team member. *Maintaining perspective* and *humility* can be challenges for many professionals, especially those with little experience; yet, both of these qualities are also very important as supervisors work to create an environment in which teamwork can be achieved.

In a face-to-face environment, the components of teamwork may be achieved during individual or group meetings. In virtual or mixed environments, virtual supervisors rely on the use of electronic methods of communication to provide support to staff members. For example, a student activities department developed a cocurricular leadership program on a Desire 2 Learn (D2L) electronic course platform, which provides an avenue for students to engage in leadership training when a student's class schedule conflicts with scheduled face-to-face sessions. Due to the volume of students involved, all professional staff members in the department collaborated to facilitate this online program. When the staff coordinator was out due to illness and a colleague volunteered to monitor the program, the volunteer replacement became the quasi-supervisor of other colleagues. The volunteer role called on the person to employ virtual supervision and team coordinating roles such as sending electronic reminders to the rest of the staff in order to post and engage students in the platform discussion, prior to the start of each unit throughout the semester, and conducting necessary electronic follow-up. The role required coordinating the actions of many and following up in the absence of face-to-face communication.

Mission-Centered Effectiveness. The scope of a supervisor's responsibility extends beyond enhancing relationships and teamwork. The third tenet, mission-centered effectiveness, is a combination of two factors: mission-centered and supervisory effectiveness. The concept of *mission-centered* reflects thoughts, action, and work products that support the mission of an organization. From experience, mission-centered effectiveness has been a chief component of strategic planning in student affairs. As supervisors develop the strategic plan for their area, the plan must relate to the division and uphold the institutional mission. It is essential that a strategic plan demonstrate what a particular department or division will accomplish that will enhance the success of the institution.

According to Ellis (2001), supervisory effectiveness can be viewed along a continuum with harmful supervision at the negative end and beneficial supervision at the positive extreme. Harmful supervision extends beyond mere ineffectiveness to actually decreasing the abilities of the employee or causing psychological harm (Ellis, 2001). Harmful supervision goes beyond hurt feelings and includes any negative impact on the employee. Poor supervision is described as being ineffective without causing harm to the employee (Ellis, 2001). Poor supervision may play out as a failure to develop an effective working relationship or failure to be helpful to employees in performing their job responsibilities. In virtual supervision formats, this might be a supervisor who is detached, fails to follow up with staff, or does not respond to messages.

At the positive end of the continuum, beneficial supervision can be described as helping employees fulfill their role in order to complete the departmental goals (Ellis, 2001). Positive supervision requires engaging with supervisees to contribute to their ability to fulfill departmental roles and enabling the supervisee to contribute to institutional goals.

Alexander Astin (1985) asserts that institutions that contribute to the learning, growth, and development of students should be more highly recognized. This *value-added* or *talent development* approach of examining an institution's success has direct application to virtual supervision. Applying Astin's (1985) talent development perspective to the role of supervision suggests that good supervisors can make important contributions to the individual as well as the institution: as supervisors develop individuals and create stronger teams, they are also strengthening the talent and potential success of the institution.

Value-added supervision is characterized by supervisors who help employees maintain their perspective and build humility (Roper, 2002). In other words, successful supervision focuses on developing the employee's maturity and responsibility, while focusing on the institutional mission. By attending to each individual and learning his or her personality, communication style, and development needs, the supervisor can strengthen the contribution each employee makes to the mission of the organization. The virtual supervisor should be conscious of the totality of the supervisee's communication, including responsiveness, tone of voice (or written message), and quality of work (which includes thoroughness). Virtual supervisors should explicitly follow up with supervisees as a way of providing feedback or offering support.

New Directions for Student Services • DOI: 10.1002/ss

In any professional relationship, misunderstandings can occur. Even when communicating face to face, in real time, without delays or physical distance, there is no guarantee that all communication is clear and easy to understand. Both the individual sending the message and the individual receiving the message need to agree on its contents for true understanding to take place (Robbins and Judge, 2007). For example, a virtual supervisor held a department meeting using videoconference software that included a Microsoft PowerPoint presentation of the key points for discussion, deadlines, and detailed information for a new project of tracking student satisfaction in cocurricular programs. The staff members who were unable to attend the meeting were sent an electronic copy of the PowerPoint presentation used during the meeting. There was no direct follow-up with the individuals to ensure that they understood the expectations. The failure to follow up caused some confusion and missed deadlines. To address this problem, the virtual supervisor followed up with the employees via phone to clarify the details of the PowerPoint document and verify understanding of expectations.

The goal of the virtual supervisor should be to create a talented team that is clear about what its specific contributions will be to the institution mission, and that communicates well as it carries out its responsibilities.

Critical Responsibilities

Critical responsibilities for student affairs supervisors include providing expectations for an employee's position, training, and evaluation. A variety of approaches exists to address each of these areas in mixed or virtual settings.

Provide Expectations. The supervisor is responsible for providing instructions and expectations when new goals or projects arise. A lack of in-person communication requires the virtual supervisor to adopt different strategies than those used by supervisors in face-to-face settings.

In the D2L student affairs leadership development program mentioned earlier, the supervisor was responsible for providing detailed instructions and expectations to facilitate student engagement in the leadership program. This included describing how often supervisees are to engage in discussion, as well as additional tips to promote student discussion on the weekly topic. Unfortunately, no area of the virtual work platform is completely error free, and even written instructions can be misleading or misunderstood.

In the example provided earlier, not all the professional staff involved understood the distinction between the main page announcement area and the discussion topic area. To clarify the appropriate procedure for where to post announcements, the virtual supervisor sent a copy of a screen shot, which is a picture of the computer screen, via email to the employee. This screen shot provided a visual identification to aid the employee in

NEW DIRECTIONS FOR STUDENT SERVICES • DOI: 10.1002/ss

understanding the location and detail of how to engage students in the leadership discussion.

Training. As Woodard, Love, and Komives (2000) suggest, change is nothing new to higher education. Therefore, a second critical responsibility for student affairs supervision is ensuring that staff have the proper information and training to complete required components of their positions, particularly in environments characterized by change.

For example, when the federal government specifies new protocols for tracking financial aid or recording crimes and safety statistics, the supervisors are responsible for ensuring that this will be accomplished. In some cases, providing training on how to address these areas is necessary. To accomplish this in a face-to-face setting, training might include a PowerPoint presentation. A virtual supervisor may not only develop a PowerPoint presentation, but also record a video of the presentation using special software to create screen-based video content (such as Adobe Captivate or TechSmith Camtasia) that allows the user to provide a voice-over along with the PowerPoint presentation.

When learning outcomes from the training program are required, corresponding tests can be developed. The status of training completion and employee achievement on related tests can be further specified. This is particularly useful when complying with federal mandates. The virtual supervisor can demonstrate the percentage of employee participation and their achievement of learning outcomes. For example, one university developed sexual harassment training to comply with sexual assault guidelines specified by the state Department of Education. Multiple versions of proficiency test questions on a given topic were developed. Therefore, training participants can retake portions of the training and receive different tests as needed. This allows employees to achieve the required 100 percent learning outcome goal of understanding the requirements for the sexual harassment training.

Evaluation. Employees should know how well they are doing in their roles. In fact, it can become a challenge to a supervisee's confidence if he believes that he is doing everything he can to meet the position requirements, only to find out that his supervisor is unhappy with his performance. This demonstrates the need for supervisors to be clear with their expectations of employee performance. Virtual supervisors can provide an operational, step-by-step guide for major performance areas. For example, federal mandates require nationwide consistency in tracking and reporting crimes. Virtual supervisors can provide a detailed operational guide in Portable Document Format (PDF) that specifies how to record and support multiple crime scenarios and corresponding responses for all areas of the campus. Such a guide would allow for a clear understanding of position requirements, relative to reporting, as well as specify the virtual supervisor's expectations.

Employee's Self-Evaluation. If the supervisor is to determine where the employee is excelling and where additional instruction or supports are

New Directions for Student Services • DOI: 10.1002/ss

needed, she should obtain the employee's perceptions of his effectiveness. This step in the evaluation process encourages the employee to be both self-reflective and self-critical of his performance (Woodard, Love, and Komives, 2000). Self-evaluation also encourages personal development and continuous learning (Reisser, 2002). In fact, Dalton and Trexler cite Blimling's list of "blunders of student affairs professionals" in *The Art and Practical Wisdom of Student Affairs Leadership* (2002). This list of blunders includes "authority without stewardship" as a mistake that can be avoided. Providing an evaluation of an employee's performance without first seeking his or her input represents a lacks of effective stewardship.

If the institution's human resources department does not require self-evaluations, a virtual supervisor can develop a form using specified performance criteria, and allow employees to self-rate their performance in each category. Once employees complete their self-evaluation, the virtual supervisor has a document to help understand the employees' assessment of their own work performance. With the employees' input, details and implications of their performance will be clearer. This self-evaluation will help address potential gaps in expected performance and actual employee performance in critical areas.

Even with the added perspective of an employee's self-evaluation in hand, there will be occasions when a virtual supervisor will require changes in the employee's performance. To address and clarify expected changes, the virtual supervisor can provide supplemental material to outline the requirements. One approach is to use free video software such as Adobe Jing to develop a video voice-over with a screen shot of the document to point out key information.

Implications for Supervisors

Perhaps one of the most unique aspects of working in student affairs is the variety of responsibilities within the field and the unique nature of working with a wide range of personalities and backgrounds. Supervisors have a pivotal role to contribute to others and the institution. Supervisors must create environments in which relationships, teamwork, and mission-centered effectiveness are incorporated with the critical factors of instruction, training, and evaluation. Virtual supervisors need specific skills and strategies in order to negotiate the challenges of virtual supervision.

Communication in the virtual environment is primarily conducted as a series of one-way messages in either a text, audio, or audiovisual format (Robbins and Judge, 2007). Virtual supervisors also use additional technologies and incorporate verbal intonation via phone or Web conference to enable the employee to accurately receive the information. Other methods for communication, using various technologies including hardware and software tools, will continue to grow as technologies change rapidly (Robbins and Judge, 2007).

NEW DIRECTIONS FOR STUDENT SERVICES • DOI: 10.1002/ss

Develop a Personal Communication Plan. Develop a comprehensive plan for communicating with staff. Determine and share in advance the expectations for virtual meetings, phone conferences, anticipated deliverables such as weekly or monthly reports, or other preferences for how you wish to communicate with supervisees. Clarify the frequency with which you will require meetings. For example, set up a monthly or regularly scheduled conference call or provide a bimonthly or quarterly video webinar. Also, indicate the expectations for checking email and voicemail. Notify your supervisees in advance of any temporary changes in communication—for example, if you are on vacation or are attending to a family illness.

Supervisors also should avail themselves of multiple ways of conversing with supervisees: text, instant message, email, and phone or Web conference. Robbins and Judge (2007) indicate that knowledge management is a skill that needs to be developed. If a supervisor does not respond to messages as questions arise, employees might become discouraged or have difficulty completing work tasks. By engaging in regular communication, the supervisor is able to contribute to the knowledge development and work performance, and enhance the connection of the supervisee to the institution. When supervisors consistently follow up on both messages and delegated tasks, this supports the employee's ability to achieve goals. According to Ramsey (1989, p. 3), "you are only as good as the people who work for you and they are only as good as you allow and equip them to be." Therefore, the success of the employee and the virtual supervisor are inextricably linked. Employing a consistent method for managing the influx of information and responding to staff is crucial for both the employee and the supervisor to accomplish their goals.

Netiquette. Netiquette is the use of good communication etiquette via electronic and typed methods such as texting or email, or during Web conferences (Shea, 1994). Using polite typed information demonstrates a professional, yet friendly, environment and fosters mutual respect. Components of netiquette may include avoiding using CAPS in typed messages and using short directives without explanation (Shea, 1994). I recommend using *please* and *thank you* consistently to provide courtesy and professionalism. If a more direct clarification is required, using a telephone or videoconference to communicate with the individuals involved might be more effective. Also, provide coaching, visual examples for guidance on specific operational tasks, and application of emotional intelligence (described later in this chapter) when needed, as these behaviors can enhance virtual supervision.

Coaching. Coaching, as described by Whitworth, Kimsey-House, and Sandahl (1998), uses positive feedback, inquiry, reflection, and instruction. These components of coaching may be applied independently or in combination to help employees. Supervisory coaching functions similarly to athletic coaching: the supervisor observes and encourages intensity and focus during practice in order to refine the team members' individual skills and performance. When a supervisor coaches an employee, he or she is looking to aid the individual in improving in specific areas of performance. This may involve listening as well as offering encouragement to the employee. Coaching can be conducted using virtual methods such as email, phone conversation, or Web conference.

Visual Aids. There are unlimited visual aids that can help clarify important concepts. Visual aids may include videos, screen shots, email attachments, or a list of bullet points within an email message. The use of visuals may also help communicate how to break down projects into smaller tasks. Visuals can provide concrete examples to guide performance.

Operational Tasks. Helping employees understand operational tasks can take the form of a myriad of strategies and may include flowcharts, forms, or any format that divides large or complex processes into smaller, understandable tasks. For example, if the dean for student conduct were developing a training program for conduct officers in a multicampus system, a helpful visual example would be to develop a flowchart for the required steps in a judicial hearing. This tool can be shared electronically and utilized as part of a larger discussion on requirements for adjudicating student conduct hearings. In this example, the virtual supervisor supports staff performance by breaking down a complex process into discrete, manageable parts.

Emotional Intelligence. Goleman (1995) indicates that there are five dimensions of emotional intelligence (EI): self-awareness, self-management, self-motivation, empathy, and social skills. Although the strategies for expanding these five dimensions of EI may not differ in a virtual setting, practice dictates that EI may be called on more frequently as the reliance on one-way communication provides the potential for communication gaps (Robbins and Judge, 2007). As a virtual supervisor, it is important to develop and enhance your own EI to recognize and understand the impact of emotions on communication and relationships in the workplace.

Conclusion

Virtual supervisors can be effective when they use professional knowledge, emotional intelligence, and adaptive tools and techniques. The tenets of supervision in student affairs and critical tasks of virtual supervision are most assuredly influenced by the nature and volume of one-way messages; misunderstandings are bound to occur. A virtual supervisor should strive to balance relationships, teamwork, and talent development with the critical tasks of providing instruction, training, and evaluation in order to further the goals and mission of his or her department, division, or institution.

As reliance on technology grows, so, too, does the need to learn the benefits and intricacies of new software programs and new hardware.

Effective virtual supervision requires ongoing training to understand the capabilities of new technologies and to expand one's skills. In order to enhance the knowledge of virtual supervisors, virtual supervision must gain more prominence as an area of professional development in student affairs. The inclusion of new technologies and strategies for applying technology to practice will become even more integral to the advancement of student affairs practice and supervision. With the ideal goal of encouraging supervisee success, the virtual supervisor can provide support and fair expectations for employees; this is best done by adopting a supervisory style that incorporates netiquette, coaching, visual examples, and operational tasks in ways that support supervisee success. Fortunately, the continuous growth and expansion of technology will enable greater flexibility and opportunities for responsiveness between the employee and virtual supervisor.

Sandeen (Dalton and Trexler, 2002) provides an important caution that has relevance for the virtual supervisor: "Technology is dazzling and mesmerizing. But student affairs' main agenda is not efficient service; it is leadership, interpersonal relations, values and effective service." There is a rightful place for technology to enhance the communication and understanding of the mission of student affairs, but an emotionally intelligent perspective ensures that technology does not impede the intuition, judgment, and interpersonal connections required to be an engaged, supportive, and responsive supervisor.

In the next chapter, Larry Roper adds to the exploration of creating positive relationships, building effective teams, and contributing to the mission of our institutions as he explores diversity and multiculturalism. He looks at the supervisor's role in building positive and diverse work groups.

References

Allen, I. E., and Seaman, J. *Learning on Demand: Online Education in the United States.* Babson Park, Mass.: Babson Survey Research Group, 2010.

Astin, A. W. *Achieving Educational Excellence: A Critical Assessment of Priorities and Practices in Higher Education.* San Francisco: Jossey-Bass, 1985.

Auer Jones, D. "Teacher Evaluation." *Chronicle of Higher Education* Review Blog, Brainstorm, Jan. 8, 2010, B2.

Bandura, A. "Modeling Theory." In W. S. Sahakian (ed.), *Learning: Systems, Models and Theories* (2nd ed., pp. 391–409). Skokie, IL: Rand McNally, 1976.

Dalton, J. C., and Trexler, A. "Nuggets of Practical Wisdom." In J. C. Dalton and M. McClinton (eds.), *The Art and Practical Wisdom of Student Affairs Leadership. New Directions for Student Services, no. 98.* San Francisco: Jossey-Bass, 2002.

DuPree, M. *Leadership Is an Art.* New York: Dell, 1989.

Ellis, M. V. "Harmful Supervision, a Cause for Alarm: Comment on Gray et al. (2001) and Nelson and Friedlander (2001)." *Journal of Counseling Psychology,* 2001, 48(4), 401–406.

Goleman, D. *Emotional Intelligence.* New York: Bantam Dell, 1995.

The Jetsons. Retrieved September 6, 2010, from http://www.tv.com/the-jetsons/show/3723/summary.html.

Presnsky, M. "Digital Natives, Digital Immigrants, Part 1." *On the Horizon*, 2001, 9(5).

Ramsey, R. D. "What Is a 'Servant Leader'?" *SuperVision*, 1989, 64(11), 3.

Reisser, L. "Self-Renewal and Personal Development in Professional Life." In J. C. Dalton and M. McClinton (eds.), *The Art and Practical Wisdom of Student Affairs Leadership. New Directions for Student Services, no. 98.* San Francisco: Jossey-Bass, 2002.

Robbins, S. P., and Judge, T. A. *Organizational Behavior.* Upper Saddle River, N.J.: Prentice Hall, 2007.

Roper, L. D. "Relationships: The Critical Ties That Bind Professionals." In J. C. Dalton and M. McClinton (eds.), *The Art and Practical Wisdom of Student Affairs Leadership. New Directions for Student Services, no. 98.* San Francisco: Jossey-Bass, 2002.

Shea, V. *Netiquette.* San Francisco, Calif.: Albion Books, 1994.

Whitworth, L., Kimsey-House, H., and Sandahl, P. *Co-Active Coaching: New Skills for Coaching People Toward Success in Work and Life.* Palo Alto, Calif.: Davies-Black, 1998.

Woodard, D. B., Love, P., and Komives, S. R. (eds). *Leadership and Management Issues for a New Century. New Directions for Student Services, no. 92.* San Francisco: Jossey-Bass, 2000.

Zenger, J. H., Musselwhite, E., Hurson, K., and Perrin, C. *Leading Teams: Mastering the New Role.* Burr Ridge, Ill.: Irwin, 1994.

Additional Resources

The following software programs were discussed in this chapter. For more information, their Web addresses are provided.

Adobe Captivate 5.5: http://www.adobe.com/products/captivate.html

Adobe Portable Document Format (PDF): http://www.adobe.com/products/acrobat/adobepdf.html

College Labs and Collegiate Link information can be retrieved from: http://www.collegiatelink.net/

Desire 2 Learn: http://www.desire2learn.com/

Facebook: http://www.facebook.com/

Microsoft PowerPoint: http://www.microsoft.com/en-us/default.aspx

TechSmith Jing: http://www.techsmith.com/jing/

TechSmith Camtasia: http://www.techsmith.com/camtasia/

Twitter: http://twitter.com/

TRISHA J. SCARCIA-KING, PHD *is director of student union and involvement services for Kutztown University and teaches multiple courses in the School of Business with Kaplan University.*

NEW DIRECTIONS FOR STUDENT SERVICES • DOI: 10.1002/ss

7

This chapter draws upon research and experiences of the author to provide insights on diversity and multiculturalism in supervision.

Supervising Across Cultures: Navigating Diversity and Multiculturalism

Larry D. Roper

Most colleges and universities have an expressed commitment to diversity. For most campuses, this means having aspirations to recruit and retain diverse students, staff, and faculty. In the process of becoming more diverse, institutions will need supervisors who can navigate the interpersonal, inter-group, and within-group relationships that come with a diverse campus.

Interaction among individuals from different cultures is an expected feature of campus life—students participate with each other in classrooms and social settings, faculties collaborate within and across disciplines, and colleagues work together to address student and campus issues. These interactions offer opportunities to enrich the lives, knowledge, and personal capacity of those involved in the exchanges, as well providing occasions to advance the work of the campus. When handled well, interactions among diverse individuals can match the ideals for diversity expressed in campus vision statements. At the same time, poorly managed interactions can create divisions and friction within organizations that might reduce the productivity of staff and limit the success of the organization.

The positive potential that exists in interactions among those from different cultures can be realized if the individuals involved in the communication possess the necessary knowledge, skills, attitudes, and commitments (Ellinor and Gerard, 1998). The focus of this chapter is to explore diversity and multiculturalism. Specifically, I will focus on how supervisors must balance the institution's diversity goals and commitments with the daily requirements to demonstrate personal multiculturalism. I will provide definitions for diversity and multiculturalism, but not devote much attention

NEW DIRECTIONS FOR STUDENT SERVICES, no. 136, Winter 2011 © Wiley Periodicals, Inc.
Published online in Wiley Online Library (wileyonlinelibrary.com) • DOI: 10.1002/ss.415

to related terms that are often part of the discussion of multiculturalism and diversity, for example, *cross-cultural* and *intercultural*. For simplicity's sake, when used in this chapter, the term *cross-cultural* is meant to convey bridging two cultural groups, while *intercultural* identifies interaction or communication among different cultural groups.

Diversity and Multiculturalism in Higher Education

Student affairs organizations are generally multicultural entities, meaning there are many different opinions, belief systems, ethnicities, races, sexual orientations, primary languages, approaches to problem solving, lifestyles, and life histories represented. The multicultural nature of student affairs makes it essential that supervisors have the ability to effectively lead and supervise in a multicultural context. For example, it is not uncommon for a student affairs work group to be comprised of persons of different ethnic backgrounds, gender identities, sexual orientations, or national origins. In such a group, the supervisor should have the ability to work and communicate effectively with all members of the group—to work across cultures.

Cross-cultural supervision is made even more challenging by the diversity among institutions and the missions of those institutions. Each college and university has a unique mission and values, which likely translates into a particular institutional culture—the institution's distinctive approach to achieving its mission and values. The differentiation in culture among colleges and universities means each campus will operate by contextually defined norms, expectations, traditions, and policies and procedures in pursuit of its desired organizational outcomes. For example, the culture of a small, faith-based liberal arts college will likely differ from a 40,000-student land-grant university. Additionally, institutions will have unique philosophies that will be informed by beliefs about the role of education, the responsibilities of educators, and the human potential of their community members (Kuh, Schuh, Whitt, and Associates, 1991).

Student affairs professionals must have the ability to navigate both institutional and individual differences *and* individual culture and institutional culture to achieve success.

In this instance, I use the definition of *culture* offered by Cupach and Canary (2000): ". . . a group-level construct that embodies a distinctive system of tradition, beliefs, values, norms, rituals, symbols and meanings that is shared by a majority of interacting individuals in a community" (p. 124). The successful student affairs supervisor must make sense of the culture of his or her campus and manage expectations and responsibilities consistent with the prevailing culture. Specifically, supervisors should be aware of the campus norms for supervision and any dominant campus beliefs regarding supervisor–supervisee relationships. For example, is the campus hierarchical? Is there strong belief in following a chain of command, and what is the expected approach to documenting performance concerns? Successful

NEW DIRECTIONS FOR STUDENT SERVICES • DOI: 10.1002/ss

supervisors will understand their campus culture and demonstrate competence in navigating that culture.

Success as a student affairs supervisor is not just a matter of understanding the culture on one's campus; it is also vital to developing competence in working with individuals from different cultural backgrounds. Developing multicultural competence is an important goal for those wishing to be successful in their supervision. Much has been written to make the case for developing the skills needed to supervise in a multicultural organization (Pope, Reynolds, and Mueller, 2004; Talbot, 2003; White and Henderson, 2008). Those who make a case for developing multicultural competence base their assertions on the professional and ethical responsibilities supervisors have to promote the success of others, as well as the obligation to help institutions navigate through complex change.

According to Curry, Wergin, and Associates (1993):

> All professionals are obligated to both acquire and to maintain the expertise needed to undertake their professional tasks, and all are obligated to undertake only those tasks that are within their competence. (p. 169)

In other words, it is the responsibility of student affairs supervisors to acquire the knowledge and skills needed to supervise the staff for which they are responsible. If one does not understand the cultural backgrounds of supervisees, the supervisor should commit to seeking out professional development to enhance supervisory effectiveness. Determining what is sufficient to designate a professional as competent, however, is a complex matter and not capable of being explored in this chapter. However, for those in supervisory roles, it is important to acknowledge the responsibility to be competent in supervision, regardless of the cultural background from which the supervisor or supervisee comes.

The remainder of this chapter will explore diversity and multiculturalism, how they are manifested, the ways they affect institutional life, and how they might be considered within the context of supervision and supervisor–supervisee relationships.

Diversity and Multiculturalism in Student Affairs

Diversity has been defined as encompassing such dimensions as race, ethnicity, gender, sexual orientation, socioeconomic status, age, physical and mental abilities, religious and political beliefs, language, and other life situations (for example, veteran status, marital status). When a supervisor embraces diversity, that individual acknowledges the presence of individuals representing a range of different attributes and characteristics (Talbot, 2003). Historically, definitions of diversity tended to focus on race, but over time the definition evolved to include other human attributes (Thomas, 1996). The definition of multiculturalism uses culture as the standard around which it is organized. The concept of multiculturalism suggests that individuals are comfortable interacting and communicating with individuals from a variety of cultures. Multiculturalism also implies that multicultural skills can be developed by exploring one's own cultural assumptions, gaining understanding of the worldviews of others, and developing appropriate behaviors and expressions to reflect one's knowledge of other cultures (White and Henderson, 2008). In her discussion of multiculturalism, Talbot (2003) asserts:

> An assumption embedded in this definition [multiculturalism] should not be overlooked nor taken for granted—it assumes that the journey toward multiculturalism is an ongoing, developmental process that can be learned. (p. 426)

Diversity refers to the ways in which people differ within and between groups, while multiculturalism refers to a person's capacity to successfully manage relationships and complex interactions with individuals from various cultures. Supervisors must understand both—how to acknowledge individual and group differences and how to manage relationships with those of different cultures.

Since the 1960s, the focus on diversity and multiculturalism has grown in importance and evolved in its complexity. Though a handful of institutions directly addressed issues of diversity early in their histories, most institutions did not mention diversity as an aspect of their institutional mission until well beyond the onset of the Civil Rights era. Initially, the most visible diversity challenges to confront colleges and universities were related to the challenges of becoming coeducational and achieving racial integration to comply with the federal mandate to desegregate public institutions. However, over time, other aspects of diversity such as sexual orientation and disability have grown in importance on campus.

While race, gender, sexual orientation, and disability have influenced the functioning of colleges and universities, campus cultures also have been influenced by such human diversity characteristics and institutional priorities as the greater inclusion and participation of low-income students, the growing numbers of international students, and the increased participation of veterans and older-than-average students. Growing diversity on campus resulted in a dramatic change in the mix of individuals represented on campus and the interpersonal interaction among those diverse people.

The profiles of student, faculty, and staff populations on most campuses differ greatly from those that would have been found fifty years ago. This can be seen most noticeably by looking at the number of institutions that have desegregated and become coeducational during that time. At the same time, the types of colleges and universities available to attend have also diversified, including private faith-based, private secular, publicly funded open access, publicly funded selective, community and technical, tribal colleges, Hispanic-serving institutions, historically black colleges and universities, single-sex, proprietary, online, and other types (Hurtado, 2003). These diverse settings are also environments in which student affairs practice and supervision take place. It is important for supervisors to understand the history and context on their campus relative to its focus on diversity.

The changes in diversity experienced by colleges and universities over the past half-century is an important factors influencing the performance of student affairs supervisors. These changes will influence student affairs professionals' responsibility to understand and respond to those with whom they work, as well as to demonstrate understanding of the institutional culture in which the professional works. Supervisors must exhibit an understanding of diversity, show the ability to be multicultural in their relationships, and act in accordance with the culture of their college or university.

Diversity, Multiculturalism, and Institutional Culture

Earlier in this chapter, the following definition of *culture* was provided: ". . . a group-level construct that embodies a distinctive system of tradition, beliefs, values, norms, rituals, symbols and meanings that is shared by a majority of interacting individuals in a community" (Cupach and Canary, 2000, p. 124). In other words, a culture is defined as a particular group's agreed-upon unique traditions, customs, beliefs, and ways of interacting with each other. A culture creates expectations for behaviors and ways of being with each other. While definitions of *culture* are helpful for understanding the components of culture, the definitions fail to describe the complexities associated with providing avenues for meaningful participation and success for those who fall outside of the majority culture. In simplest terms, the definition of *culture* suggests a "majority rules" view of how organizations function—the norms and expectations are defined by what the majority agrees upon.

Supervisors have responsibility for promoting the growth and success of members of the campus community for whom some of the agreed-upon values, norms, traditions, and meanings do not make sense. If a campus truly has diversity in its workforce, there will be supervisees whose lives are guided by a range of norms, values, and traditions. The obligation of a supervisor is to promote supervisee growth and development, balanced with holding the supervisee accountable for demonstrating successful performance in the staff member's assigned position. Supervisors must ensure that those whom they supervise perform their responsibilities in an effective and efficient manner (Dalton, 2003). Thus, this is the challenge of diversity and multiculturalism: how does one demonstrate an understanding and appreciation of the uniqueness of each supervisee while at the same time showing the ability to hold that same supervisee accountable for meeting expectations that are informed by the cultural norms of the campus?

New Directions for Student Services • DOI: 10.1002/ss

Impact of Diversity and Multiculturalism on Supervisors

The kinds of diversity represented in an organization will influence the complexity of issues encountered by supervisors (Thomas, 1996). Because diversity has many dimensions to it and because culture is multifaceted, there should be little doubt why supervisors will find navigating diversity and developing multiculturalism challenging propositions. While supervisors might be inclined to want to focus on either diversity or multiculturalism, in supervisory relationships it is virtually impossible to deal with them separately. In the context of supervision, knowledge of diversity allows the supervisor to recognize and appreciate the differences among and within individuals, while multiculturalism offers the requirement that the supervisor demonstrate the ability to construct and carry out successful relationships with those from different cultures. Even as diversity and multiculturalism are important individually, for supervisors they must be viewed as integrated concepts.

Many student affairs supervisors are posed with providing supervision for supervisees who are different than they are in terms of age, physical and mental ability, disability, cultural background, sexual orientation, gender, beliefs and religion, primary language, and other factors. The expectation that one should provide multicultural supervision might result in some supervisors' increasing their awareness of the similarities and differences between the supervisor and the supervisee, while others might pretend or lead themselves to believe no differences exist. It is not unusual that a supervisor may be keenly aware of some aspects of diversity, yet be unable to discern the presence of other forms of diversity. Supervisors must be able to recognize differences so that they can better respond to and facilitate individual and group dynamics effectively (Thomas, 1996). Recognizing differences allows a supervisor respond to experiences a supervisee might have that are outside the realm of the supervisor's own life experiences. For example, a male supervisor might believe there are no differences in the experiences of men and women in the organization. However, when the supervisor increases his awareness of gender differences, he becomes much more aware of how sexism influences the experiences of female supervisees. This new knowledge can then guide the supervisor in learning how to be of support to female supervisees. Also, when the supervisor acknowledges to the supervisee his increased understanding of gender dynamics and its impact on the supervisee, it can create an opportunity for improved communication and relating between the supervisor and supervisee. When a supervisor communicates awareness of diversity, while also exhibiting multicultural competence, the supervisor is better situated to develop a more inclusive organization, as well as support improved performance by supervisees (Pope et al., 2004).

Equally as important as a supervisor's recognizing differences in others is that the supervisor commit to understanding his own personal experiences and how those experiences affect his ability to interact with others in ways that allow the other person to feel respected. For example, White and Henderson (2008) suggest that mental health professionals can enhance their self-awareness by: (1) exploring their own ethnic background and how their background influences their beliefs, outlook, and knowledge of self; (2) understanding the advantages and disadvantages associated with the various identity groups to which they belong (for example, race, gender, religion, ability); (3) cultivate awareness of a critical life incident in which they experienced the power of the dominant social culture; and (4) get in touch with an experience they had with being discriminated against, excluded, or persecuted. By undergoing this level of self-exploration, the supervisor might gain insight into his own strengths and challenges, relative to supervising in a multicultural organization.

It is important for supervisors to engage in this level of personal exploration so that they can recognize how their own culture might influence how they interact with individuals from different cultural backgrounds. By understanding the privileges associated with the different identity groups to which they belong, supervisors might also better understand how supervisees might be disadvantaged by groups to which they belong. By being in touch with how one's life has been influenced by the dominant culture, supervisors can better understand the potential impact of the power associated with their position. Finally, supervisors can develop empathy for what supervisees might experience by reflecting on situations in which the supervisor felt the impact of not being acknowledged. Effective supervision requires not just an awareness of the attributes the supervisee brings to the relationship, but also knowledge of the characteristics the supervisor contributes to the relationship.

Self-awareness can bring into clarity the supervisor's cultural assumptions, which might be helpful in determining areas for future learning and professional development. Because of the ever-changing nature of diversity, the development of multicultural competence should be viewed as a lifelong process (Pope et al., 2004). By committing to professional development, supervisors demonstrate their desire to increase their effectiveness with supervisees whose backgrounds are different than theirs.

The supervisor should attempt to understand the individual situation of each supervisee, including the supervisee's perspective on work, his or her cultural background and assumptions, and what the supervisee regards as pivotal experiences in his or her own background. Also, understanding supervisees' preferred learning style and leadership preferences can provide the supervisor with important insights into staff members' strengths and challenges. For example, knowledge that a supervisee prefers to learn through concrete examples may be beneficial in determining how to help that supervisee improve his or her performance. In many organizations, instruments such as the Myers-Briggs Type Indicator have been used to assess supervisees' preference for the structure of work environments, relationships, and experiences (Barger and Kirby, 1995). Such an assessment tool is helpful to supervisors in determining how to design professional development experiences and how to utilize a supervisee's work preferences in assigning roles.

Conflict within work groups can often arise from staff members' not understanding or appreciating the different approaches to work, thinking, and group participation preferences that exist within a group of colleagues. StrengthsQuest has been widely used by college and university leaders to better understand preferred leadership styles of staff at all levels of the organization (StrengthsQuest, 2010). The value of an instrument such as StrengthsQuest lies in its ability to identify a supervisee's talents and offer examples of how the supervisee might utilize her or his talents to achieve work success. Supervisors might use an instrument of this type to build appreciation of talent within the work group and to understand where potential conflicts among supervisees' strengths might arise. By understanding the individual work preferences of supervisees and the mix of preferences within a group, the supervisor can then consider how to support individual supervisees, as well as work with the diversity of styles within the group.

While supervision is generally considered an individual activity, supervisors must also work with staff groups. Individuals who share a common supervisor often come together for the purpose of staff meetings, planning, problem solving, decision making, professional development, and other activities requiring interpersonal communication, cooperation, and collaboration. Although positive and productive outcomes can result from a staff group's working together, there also can be periodic conflict, tension, or miscommunication. Conflict might arise from competing goals, competition for resources, cultural differences, power discrepancies, and expectations that members conform to group norms (Cox, 1994). Real and perceived cultural differences surface in any number of ways within work groups. As supervisors develop awareness of potential conflict that might arise from diversity within their work group, they can plan their own and the group's professional development experiences to cultivate the skills needed to manage or avert conflict situations.

Whenever individuals gather for the purpose of work, there is a potential for power discrepancies to emerge. Supervisees often expect the supervisor to be the one to resolve differences and ensure equity in power among staff members. The perception of majority–minority power differences can be very destructive to the functioning of an organization—who gets acknowledged, who gets access to the supervisor's time, or who gets the benefit of the doubt when problems arise? The supervisor must develop an approach to supervision that models acknowledgment of the efforts of each supervisee, offers equal supervisory and mentoring access to all supervisees, and provides fair consideration for all when problematic issues occur. As the supervisor is working to be fair and equitable, he or she must also work to respond to the unique needs each supervisee brings. This can be difficult, as the supervisor works to balance attention to group norms as well as individual needs.

When supervisors make allowances for the unique needs of a particular supervisee, others may feel the accommodation has a detrimental impact on them. When a supervisee shows distinctive needs, the supervisor is confronted with demonstrating the ability to acknowledge those differences. Whatever the supervisor decides, he or she will likely be called on to justify the decision. Consider the case of accommodation of a supervisee with disabilities. To what degree do other supervisees resent the impact of the accommodation on them? Do they believe the financial resources invested in the accommodation should have been available for their program, or do they believe the person with disabilities should have to "tough it out"? Even when the diverse needs of a supervisee are clearly documented, response to those needs can be a source of tension in work groups. In work groups, conformity and diversity can be a constant source of friction for the supervisor and supervisees.

With all of the potential challenges inherent in work groups, it is important for supervisors to have a clear vision of the positive potential that can be realized by creating a work group that is capable of communicating well, resolving conflicts, acknowledging and supporting the needs of members, and working with each other in a way that demonstrates respect for each person's cultural background. While the research is very clear that diverse workgroups have more creative potential than monocultural groups, that potential will not be realized without skillful supervision, leadership, and facilitation (Cox, 1994; Ellinor and Gerard, 1998; Thomas, 1996). To be effective, supervisors should be able to build a work group that demonstrates support for the individual differences of members while at the same time developing a strong sense of community. Feelings of community (common good) emerge from creating shared values, vision, and purposes within a group (Love and Estanek, 2004). When a work group functions as a community, the effectiveness of the group will be evident in greater risk taking, more successful communication, increased learning and information sharing, and a more dynamic work environment.

Cox (1994) suggests there are moral and ethical reasons for why supervisors must develop the skills needed to manage the responsibilities and expectations that come with organizational diversity. In Cox's view, supervisors have a moral responsibility to understand who their supervisees are, the particular needs they bring to the workplace, and what is needed on behalf of the supervisor to support the supervisee's success in his or her job. It is immoral and unethical for a supervisor to not know or to disregard a supervisee's unique personal situation.

Even when a supervisor understands his or her supervisees, diversity is a challenging issue to manage in interpersonal relationships and organizational life. Ellinor and Gerard (1998) suggest:

Diversity is a huge dilemma and question for our species. We want to believe that all our diverse perspectives are necessary to the health of our whole, our community. At the same time, all of us want to be right about how we see the world. (p. 277)

The preceding quote suggests that many people will struggle with diversity. While individuals might value diversity, they might also struggle with looking at issues from perspectives different than their own. Supervisors are put in the role of having to support the belief that diverse views are necessary, while also managing their inclination to assert their own cultural views.

Each member of the work group brings his or her own identity and socialization to the supervisory relationship. Therefore, in one-on-one interactions and in groups, the supervisor and supervisees should be cognizant of how their backgrounds influence their ability to communicate and work with each other. Supervisors and supervisees should build in time to discuss areas where each might improve their ability to contribute positively to the diversity of the work group. Too often, conversations of this nature are avoided because there are high stakes associated with such conversations. For example, if a supervisor were to reveal to a gay supervisee that he or she was raised in a household where the belief was cultivated that homosexuality is a sin and gay people should not be allowed to be around young people, the supervisor would likely wonder if sharing such information would compromise her or his credibility. Often, fear of losing credibility or social standing can be an obstacle to both supervisors and supervisees sharing information that might ultimately lead to a better supervisor–supervisee relationship and stronger community within the work group.

Imagine the anxiety a supervisor might experience if she or he were to approach a conversation with a supervisee by asking, "Do you think it would be helpful if we were to talk about what it might mean for our work relationship that I am a heterosexual, white female, and you are a gay, Latino male?" or "Can you help me to understand issues that I as a Japanese, male administrator need to better understand about you as a blind, female, African American, Gulf War veteran in order for me to be a good supervisor for you?" First, it is difficult to determine how to initiate the conversation, which in some cases means making assumptions about what identity is most salient for the other person. Second is the challenge of finding the humility necessary to reveal to the supervisee that there are areas where you might need help or where you do not have sufficient knowledge or awareness to support the supervisee's development.

Supervisors should invest in developing the necessary skills to initiate and manage potentially difficult conversations that are important to demonstrate multiculturalism. Supervisors should take advantage of professional development opportunities offered through professional associations, which might require participating in conferences and institutes outside the realm of one's usual professional involvement.

In order to build the desired relationship with supervisees, supervisors might have to overcome the social norm in the United States to be "color-blind" and not notice differences (Dyson, 1997; Helms, 1992). Some supervisors might have been socialized that it is not polite to notice differences. In an effort to see every person as "just another human being," supervisors can fail to recognize attributes that are significant in a supervisee's approach to relationships and organizational life. When supervisors do not observe differences, they overlook characteristics that may be very important to supervisees, such as race, gender, disability, veteran status, or other personal attributes. To look at all people as being the same might appear to reflect open-mindedness, but in supervisory roles, such an approach can result in overlooking personal characteristics that are essential to the success of individuals, groups, and the organization. A supervisor who has achieved competence in multiculturalism will acknowledge the diversity within those he or she supervises and demonstrate the ability to carry out relationships of respect, appreciation, and support.

Conclusion

Successful supervision involves constructing a relationship between the supervisor and supervisee that promotes job success for the supervisee. Diversity can often add challenges to the supervisor–supervisee relationship. However, if the supervisor cultivates an environment that allows her or him and supervisees to openly explore issues of diversity and develop their multiculturalism, diversity can serve as a positive element in the work group.

Supervisors who truly embrace diversity and commit themselves to exhibiting multiculturalism will not only achieve success in supervision and relationships, but will model for others the ideals of how multicultural communities should function. In that regard, supervision goes beyond what one does in his or her one-on-one relationships with supervisees—it extends to the responsibility supervisors have to shape the culture of the campus community. A good supervisor not only influences the lives of supervisees, but can potentially have a profound impact on those beyond their immediate work group by virtue of their ability to navigate the multicultural landscape of the campus.

The multicultural supervisor is able to move with ease into and out of different cultural contexts, creating a history of culture-affirming relationships as he or she goes. In the process of constructing positive supervisory relationships, the supervisor will add substantively to the mission of the campus.

In the chapter that follows, Lori White will touch on issues of diversity and other challenges facing midlevel supervisors. Through the use of case studies, the author will guide the reader through scenarios with elements common to student affairs supervision.

References

Barger, N. J., and Kirby, L. K. *The Challenge of Change in Organizations: Helping Supervisees Thrive in the New Frontier*. Palo Alto, CA: Davies-Black, 1995.

Cox, T., Jr. *Cultural Diversity in Organizations Theory, Research, and Practice*. San Francisco: Berrett-Koehler, 1994.

Cupach, W. R., and Canary, D. J. *Competence in Interpersonal Conflict*. Long Grove, Ill.: Waveland Press, 2000.

Curry, L., Wergin, J. F., and Associates. *Educating Professionals: Responding to New Expectations for Competence and Accountability*. San Francisco: Jossey-Bass, 1993.

Dalton, J. C. "Managing Human Resources." In Komives, S. R., Woodard D. B. Jr., and Associates (eds.), *Student Services: A Handbook for the Profession* (pp. 397–419). San Francisco: Jossey-Bass, 2003.

Dyson, M. E. *Race Rules: Navigating the Color Line*. New York: Vintage Books, 1997.

Ellinor, L., and Gerard, G. *Dialogue: Rediscover the Transforming Power of Conversation*. New York: John Wiley & Sons, 1998.

Helms, J. E. *A Race Is a Nice Thing to Have: A Guide to Being a White Person or Understanding the White Person in Your Life*. Topeka, Kan.: Content Communications, 1992.

Hurtado, S. "Institutional Diversity in American Higher Education." In Komives, S. R., Woodard D. B. Jr., and Associates (eds.), *Student Services: A Handbook for the Profession* (pp. 23–44). San Francisco: Jossey-Bass, 2003.

Kuh, G. D., Schuh, J. H., Whitt, E. J., and Associates. *Involving Colleges: Successful Approaches to Fostering Student Learning and Development Outside the Classroom*. San Francisco: Jossey-Bass, 1991.

Love, P. G., and Estanek, S. M. *Rethinking Student Affairs Practice*. San Francisco: Jossey-Bass, 2004.

Pope, R. L., Reynolds, A. L., and Mueller, J. A. *Multicultural Competence in Student Affairs*. San Francisco: Jossey-Bass, 2004.

StrenghtsQuest. Gallup, Inc. Accessed September 30, 2010, at https://www.strengthsquest.com/.

Talbot, D. M. "Multiculturalism." In Komives, S. R., Woodard D. B. Jr., and Associates (eds.), *Student Services: A Handbook for the Profession* (pp. 423–446). San Francisco: Jossey-Bass, 2003.

Thomas, R. R., Jr. *Redefining Diversity*. New York: AMACON, 1996.

White, J. L., and Henderson, S. J. *Building Multicultural Competency: Development, Training, and Practice*. Lanham, Md.: Rowan & Littlefield, 2008.

LARRY D. ROPER is vice provost for student affairs and professor of ethnic studies at Oregon State University.

*The author uses case studies to explore challenging
supervisory situations and draws upon her experience to
suggest possible approaches.*

8

Case Studies in Middle Management Supervision

Lori S. White

The previous chapters have provided an overview of the complexities of supervision. This chapter presents a series of supervision-related case studies of situations that midlevel managers might face.

Individuals enrolled in a midlevel management professional development course recommended the topics selected for this chapter. Drawing upon my experience teaching the course, I selected four case studies that individuals in the class found most helpful to their work and/or evoked some of our most lively discussions. The case studies outlined in this chapter are designed to stimulate discussions about the cases themselves and to offer my professional perspective on how I might respond to the cases, if presented with similar scenarios. Embedded throughout each of the cases, and in the discussion section that follows each case study, is a series of questions for the reader to ponder.

The perspectives I offer related to each of the case studies presented are through the lens of someone who identifies herself as a "Baby Boomer," African American, female, Vice President of Student Affairs. In my 30-plus years of working in higher education, I have worked at both public and private universities (all four-year institutions) and have supervised many of the traditional student affairs areas such as residence life, new-student programs, student health and counseling, the career development center, recreational sports, multicultural student affairs, and student activities. Other senior-level managers in student affairs with different backgrounds and experiences might approach the case studies differently. Thus, the case studies are offered as a means of encouraging discussion about the various

NEW DIRECTIONS FOR STUDENT SERVICES, no. 136, Winter 2011 © Wiley Periodicals, Inc.
Published online in Wiley Online Library (wileyonlinelibrary.com) • DOI: 10.1002/ss.416

ways one might respond when presented with one or more of the case study scenarios.

Case Study 1

How should I approach my new role as a supervisor of professional staff?

You have been promoted from residence hall director at Western University to an assistant director of residence life. You will be supervising a staff of three hall directors and an administrative assistant. You know all of these individuals well because you worked with them as a hall director. However, serving as their supervisor and supervising professional (nonstudent staff) will be a new role for you. Also, one of the hall directors whom you will now be supervising was also a candidate for the position.

Reflection Questions. What are some ways you might approach this new role? As a new supervisor, where might you have challenges? In what ways might your supervisory role be affected by the fact that one of your supervisees was also a candidate for the position for which you have been hired? What resources, if any, are available to you, either at your institution or through a professional association in which you might be involved, that might be helpful to you in your supervisory role?

Discussion

Approaching the Supervisory Role. My experiences as a supervisor have led me to conclude that an effective supervisor provides the supervisee with clear expectations about the goals for the position and work performance; resources to perform the work successfully (such as a budget, office space, equipment, and training); assurances that the supervisor is personally supportive of the supervisee and has confidence in the supervisee's abilities to perform her job well; and a clear outline of how performance will be evaluated. Dalton's (2003) *Managing Human Resources* includes many of the aforementioned as core components of his supervisory model. The literature related to supervision also indicates that many supervisees want their supervisor to be a mentor (Renn and Hodges, 2007) and to assist the supervisee with the achievement of the supervisee's professional goals (cf. Stock-Ward and Javorek, 2003).

Take a minute to think about the following questions: How will you structure your conversations with each supervisee to discuss performance expectations and goals? How would you assess the extent to which resources and other support structures are in place so that the supervisee has the tools to be successful? What is your plan for evaluating the supervisee's performance, and how will the supervisee know what your evaluation process will be? To what extent do you think it important for the supervisees to know that you have confidence in their ability to do their job? If the supervisees expect you to provide mentoring and help with their respective professional goals, what ideas do you have in that regard?

Challenges for New Supervisors. While this case study indicates that you are someone who is a new supervisor, supervisory challenges are not unique to those who are new supervisors. Even those who have supervised staff for many years can find themselves having difficulty supervising an individual or a team of staff for any number of reasons. For example, issues might arise between a supervisor and his supervisees because of miscommunication about a work assignment, differences in work styles, unclear or unrealistic performance expectations, or poor work performance. This case study presents what could be a potential challenge for the supervisor, the fact that one of the new supervisees is someone who also applied for the position.

How would you transition from a peer-to-peer relationship with this individual (as well as others with whom you worked before being promoted) to a supervisor–supervisee relationship? What might be some of the potential difficulties and opportunities with respect to your supervision of a former peer?

Individuals in the midlevel management class offered a variety of suggestions in response to the potential challenge of supervising a former peer and/or someone who had also applied for the position for which one was hired. Ideas included the new supervisor's inviting the individual who applied for the position to take on a special assignment for the department or the university that capitalized on her particular strengths and emphasizing the important role she plays as a member of the work team.

I have employed the preceding strategies in similar situations. However, sometimes, despite one's best efforts, there are staff whom you are charged with supervising who are not able to adjust to the disappointment of not being selected for a position for which they and the supervisor applied. Some may have difficulty with the idea of reporting to a former peer. In these instances, discussing the issue with your supervisor and/or your human resources department may help provide you with some strategies for working with these staff members, particularly if their inability to adjust to having you as their supervisor is negatively affecting your work and that of others in your department.

Supervisory Resources. How does one learn how to supervise? In Chapter Two, Cathlene McGraw says that much of what we learn about supervision comes from our own experiences as supervisees. Most student affairs professionals can likely recall "good" and "bad" bosses and can use those experiences to guide the development of our own supervisory style and relationships with those whom we supervise. However, Stock-Ward and Javorek (2003) also encourage supervisor training so that we do not rely on past supervisory experiences as our only model for learning about how to be supervisors. This monograph provides a range of experiences and advice related to supervision, and there are a number of other resources cited in the reference section of each chapter. I also encourage you to use the training resources offered on your campus and through various higher education professional associations.

NEW DIRECTIONS FOR STUDENT SERVICES • DOI: 10.1002/ss

Case Study 2

How should I respond if I think a supervisee is engaging in poor decision making or is doing something that is unethical?

You are the associate director of the Student Health Center. Among your responsibilities is to oversee the Peer Health Education program. Samuel is the graduate assistant for your office. Samuel completed his undergraduate degree last year at the university where you are both working and where he is now working on his master's degree in student affairs. In his GA role, Samuel helps you supervise the student Peer Health Educator (PHE) program.

While you are working late one evening, you overhear the PHEs talking about Samuel. In the course of their conversation, you hear the PHEs use the words *hypocrite* and *poor professional role model* to describe Samuel. One example the students cite is the fact that Samuel has pictures on his Facebook page showing him from his undergraduate days partying with his friends (some of whom are still undergraduates at the institution). Upon accepting the position, PHEs sign a contract not to drink. You sigh when you hear this as you recall a conversation you had with Samuel about Facebook when he first started working in the office. You asked Samuel to remove anything on Facebook that would not be appropriate for a professional staff person. Samuel assured you he would take care of this right away. Unfortunately, it looks like he has not kept his word. The students also mention that Samuel, upon returning from a professional conference, told them that he ate light during the conference so he could pocket the university travel per diem for spending money for his upcoming vacation. The PHEs say that during their training both you and Samuel emphasized the importance of ethics, and they are pretty sure keeping travel funds is not ethical.

Reflection Questions. Having overheard the PHEs' conversation, what do you see as the key issues for you, as Samuel's supervisor? Since the PHEs did not discuss their concerns about Samuel with you directly, how would you respond to the situation? What, if anything, do you think should happen to Samuel related to the PHEs' concerns?

Discussion

Key Issues in Supervising Samuel. This case study was posed to the class by the person who was the associate director in the scenario, in hopes of receiving advice from classmates about how he might respond. Our class conversations about the case focused on several questions.

One question the class wanted to explore in greater depth was how a supervisor should respond to information or concerns about a supervisee that may not have been presented directly to the supervisor? The emphasis on student staff in this case study was an important supervision issue for the individuals in the midlevel management class. Many of the individuals in the class, in addition to supervising professional staff, also have responsibility for supervising graduate students, and directly or indirectly supervise a sizeable staff of student leaders (for example, resident assistants, orientation leaders, and peer educators). A second question the class wanted to discuss was what a supervisor should do when a supervisee has not followed through on a mutually agreed upon expectation or commitment. A third question focused on how a supervisor deals with a supervisee who has made poor decisions, particularly if those poor decisions also include violations of university policy.

Supervisors and Performance Management. For discussion purposes, let us assume the information about Samuel, as described by the PHEs, is accurate (later in the discussion we will talk about a supervisor's options if the supervisor has heard troubling information about a supervisee indirectly, as opposed to directly). Samuel has not followed through on something he has agreed to do—take down particular Facebook pages; has pictures of himself engaged in behavior the PHEs, whom Samuel cosupervises with you, have committed not to be a part of; and may have used university resources inappropriately.

The first case study in this chapter focused on providing a basic framework for approaching supervision of staff. However, I would also like to emphasize that supervision of staff is an ongoing, not a static, process. While there are a number of different supervisory issues in this case study related to Samuel, I would organize them all under the overall category of performance management. I define performance management as the *ongoing* direction a supervisor provides to a supervisee to ensure that a supervisee is appropriately executing his job responsibilities.

With regard to this case study, I offer four performance management strategies that you might consider as Samuel's supervisor. One is to be clear with Samuel about your performance expectations. Let Samuel (and other new employees) know upon initial hire and through your various meetings the scope of his job responsibilities and the manner in which you expect those responsibilities to be performed. For example, projects assigned should be completed in a timely manner; university policies and procedures should always be followed; and you expect him to be a role model for student staff of appropriate professional behavior in the workplace.

A second performance management strategy is for you to take any necessary steps to ensure that Samuel is meeting your performance expectations. For example, one of these steps might include checking in with Samuel regularly regarding any assignment you may have given him to make sure the assignment has been completed. The case study involving Samuel suggests that you, as Samuel's supervisor, are surprised to learn that Samuel has not taken down his Facebook page. Perhaps regular check-in meetings between Samuel and you, where the agenda includes setting deadline dates for any assigned tasks, would be a good idea. It is also important to follow through to ensure that Samuel is meeting your expectations.

New Directions for Student Services • DOI: 10.1002/ss

A third component of performance management is to make sure Samuel has a clear understanding of university policies and knows that, as his supervisor, you have a responsibility to hold him (and all other staff) accountable for understanding and complying with those policies. For example, does Samuel, as a graduate student, understand the university policies regarding travel per diem? What information and training have you or others provided to him in that regard?

Another aspect of performance management is setting the tone for the work environment. Tone setting could include anything from what expectations you have for staff attire in the office to how you expect staff to communicate problems or concerns about other staff members to you, expectations for punctuality, or how staff should approach resolving conflict.

In your interactions with current staff, what discussions have you had about how you would like to see concerns among staff resolved? In this particular case, you discovered that the student staff has some concerns about Samuel only because you overheard their conversation. What opportunities might you create for the student staff to provide you with feedback about Samuel? Given the definition of performance management presented, in what performance management strategies might you engage to supervise Samuel?

Ethical Issues in Supervision. What if it is your sense that Samuel was being untruthful about forgetting to take down his Facebook page and/or that he knew the university policies about per diem and still ignored them?

In my middle management class, we had a lot of discussion about the role of ethics in student affairs. For the purposes of this chapter, ethics is defined very generally as upholding university values, norms, standards, and policies. Ethical behavior is defined as acting in accordance with these values, norms, standards, and policies. Some institutions articulate a code of ethics. (For example, see Southern Methodist University, University Policy Manual, 1.20, University Code of Ethics, http://smu.edu/policy/.) However, I think all institutions, whether or not they have a written code of ethics, expect all members of the college or university community to demonstrate ethical behavior.

There are a number of articles specifically related to ethics in student affairs (Reybold, Halx, and Jimenez, 2008; Sundberg and Fried, 1997; Winston and Creamer, 1998). The definition of *professional ethicality* offered by Reybold and colleagues is adherence to commonly accepted principles and standards for our conduct in the workplace. Reybold and colleagues advocate strong professional ethics for individuals working in student affairs specifically because our work takes place in a higher education setting. The authors refer to higher education as a professional context that has an "unquestionable moral compass" (Wilcox and Ebbs, 1992, p. xvii, cited by Reybold et al.). Among the reasons they emphasize for high ethical standards being important for those of us who work in higher education is our roles as mentors and role models to students.

NEW DIRECTIONS FOR STUDENT SERVICES • DOI: 10.1002/ss

Collectively, the articles I have cited regarding ethics in student affairs underscore that ethical conduct (acting in ways that are consistent with commonly accepted professional standards) is a core value of student affairs work, and part of our work as professionals is to model these values to others, particularly to students.

Given the preceding definition of professional ethics, do you see Samuel's alleged behavior as an ethical issue? If so, what are the ethical issues that concern you as a supervisor? How should you respond to Samuel's behavior? What are your thoughts about the proposition that student affairs professionals have a responsibility to model ethical behavior for others, particularly for students?

A Supervisor's Dilemma: I Heard It Through the Grapevine. In the event you are not familiar with the song "I Heard It Through the Grapevine" (written by Norman Whitfield and Barrett Strong for the Motown record label), the song is about an individual who learns that his relationship is not going well, not directly from his lover, but indirectly through the gossip mill, the grapevine. Sometimes, as supervisors, we learn through a campus grapevine that others have issues with our supervisees about which we are unaware.

In class conversations about this particular case study, one of the most challenging questions with which the class wrestled was what a supervisor should do with information about a supervisee that is learned indirectly. A further complicating factor in this case study was that the indirect information came from students. Many mid-level managers, including those in my class, in addition to supervising staff, also work very closely with students. The class participants talked about how important it was to them in their supervisory roles to also have open and trusting relationships with students.

Given the case study's implication that you have overheard the students talking about Samuel, what would you do in response?

From a very general perspective, a supervisor cannot assume that *grapevine* information in the workplace about a supervisee is fact or make supervisory-related decisions based solely on hearsay information. However, if the information you hear appears to be related to any issue that may put the individual staff member, your department, or the university at risk, then I would recommend engaging your supervisor in a conversation about whether and how to discuss the issues you are hearing about with the supervisee in question.

In this case study, one critical piece of information is that you have directly overheard student staff in your office discussing concerning information about Samuel, so this is not something that has come to you second- or third-hand or through the rumor mill. It certainly would not be fair to Samuel to jump to the conclusion that the students' conversation about Samuel is altogether true or fact. However, as Samuel's supervisor, and as the supervisor of the PHEs, you should let the student PHEs know immediately you have overheard their conversation and would like to discuss their concerns about Samuel with them. The information you learn from your conversation with the PHEs might assist you in developing a performance management plan with respect to Samuel.

What if the discussion between you and the students occurs and the students ask you not to say anything to Samuel because they do not want to get him in trouble? What would you do then?

This case study suggests that the concerns the PHEs have about Samuel are very much issues of concern to them; otherwise, they might not have been spending time discussing their issues with Samuel among themselves. If the contention about student affairs staff serving as ethical role models for students is accurate, then it might follow that the PHEs look to Samuel and to you, as their supervisors, to set and to adhere to particular standards for your work and theirs. Your ability and Samuel's to meet the expectation of the student staff will be undermined if the PHEs see you and Samuel behaving in ways that are inconsistent with what they believe are the professional standards you have set for them. A particular challenge with this case is that the PHEs have asked you not to say anything to Samuel about what you overheard them discussing. However, if you were to choose not to say anything to Samuel, while also holding PHEs accountable for expectations similar to those you have for Samuel, how might this impact how the PHEs perceive your credibility as a supervisor and/or a role model?

One strategy for responding to the PHEs' request that you not tell Samuel about your conversation with them is to let the students know how seriously you take your role as an educator. Because Samuel is a graduate student in training, you can emphasize for the PHEs that, as Samuel's supervisor, you want to do everything you can to help Samuel be successful in his current position and in preparation for future job possibilities. Thus, for you to help Samuel achieve those goals, it is important for you to discuss and resolve the issues the PHEs have brought to your attention with Samuel.

What are some other reasons you might share with the students about why you would like to have a conversation with Samuel about the students' concerns? Can you think of any reasons why you should not mention to the students that you have overheard their conversation or discuss their concerns with Samuel?

The Conversation with Samuel. If you conclude that you should indeed have a conversation with Samuel about the students' concerns, how might you construct the conversation? What if Samuel does not believe that the issues about his Facebook photos and his per diem are relevant to his job performance? Would you share with Samuel the manner in which the concerns were brought to your attention?

The supervisors in the mid-level management class did not come up with any one standard approach for constructing the conversation with

Samuel (in response to the information learned from the PHEs). However, many class participants thought if they were Samuel's supervisor, they would try to keep the conversation with Samuel focused on their interest in helping Samuel be a successful student affairs professional. This is not to say they would not express disappointment to Samuel about his lack of follow-through on taking down his Facebook page or share concern that he may have not used his per diem in accordance with university policy. However, in the absence of prior performance issues, class members believed the conversation with Samuel should be developmental (focused on growth and learning) rather than punitive. Also, because the issues being discussed with Samuel were brought to the supervisor's attention by the PHEs, members of the class felt that a developmental conversation with Samuel might help mitigate any negative perceptions Samuel might have toward the PHEs for "telling" on him. The course participants also thought it important that the supervisor provide a clear time line to Samuel for cleaning up his Facebook page and to let Samuel know what the consequences would be for noncompliance. Finally, the staff in the midlevel management course thought it important that Samuel receive some additional training regarding university policies.

Other than the approaches suggested by the class, what approaches might you take in constructing the conversation with Samuel? What consequences, if any, should there be for Samuel as a result of issues brought to your attention by the PHEs?

Case Study 3

What if I have challenges related to supervising an ethnically and culturally diverse staff?

You, Stephanie, are the director of the student union, a position you have held for four years. When you assumed the position of director of the student union four years ago, most of the staff of the Student Center were white. The Center itself had a reputation as the place on campus where the white students went to hang out—with the minority and other "diverse" students on campus preferring to hang out at one of the campus cultural and/or advocacy centers (for example, the Black Student Center; Latino Student Center; Asian Student Center; Native American Student Center; Pride Center; Women's Center). As an African American woman, you are the first person of color and first woman to hold the position of the director of the student union on your campus. In fact, when you arrived on campus, most of the staff of color in the Division of Student Affairs worked in one of the campus cultural or advocacy centers. Also, there are no professionals of color at the assistant or associate director levels in the Center.

During your tenure as the director of the Student Center, you have been very vocal about the importance of the Center's being a place where all students on campus feel comfortable and welcome, and that having a diverse staff working at the Center (other than the housekeeping and maintenance staff) will help encourage more diverse student participation in the Center. Over the course of your four years as director, you have been able to hire and promote three new staff of color into various positions in the Center, including at the assistant director and associate director levels. You have also promoted other staff from within, including one white man and two white women.

One morning you receive an email message from one of your associate directors announcing a diversity workshop facilitated by the institution's human resources department. In the email, the associate director recommends that the workshop be scheduled for the professional staff in the Center as one of the professional development activities for the semester. You think this is a great idea and work with HR to arrange the workshop.

Unfortunately, the workshop turns out to be a disaster. An instant survey as part of the workshop reveals that staff think the diversity climate in the Center is horrible; that both majority and minority staff are fearful of bringing up any discussions of diversity because they do not feel safe doing so; and some staff feel that some are being hired, promoted, and retained because of a desire to fill a particular diversity quota or pursue a specific "agenda." Some supervisees feel there is too much emphasis on diversity, while others feel there is not enough emphasis on diversity.

The individual coordinating the workshop turns out to be ineffective at facilitating a discussion about the issues identified in the survey, and by the end of the workshop you could cut the tension in the room with a knife. You know that your supervisees are looking to you to help them resolve their concerns. As the supervisor of this team, what do you do?

Reflection Questions. What do you see as the key management and supervisory challenges within Case Study 3? If you were Stephanie or new to a similar position, how would you have approached the management and supervisory challenges you identified? Do you think Stephanie should or could have anticipated the outcome of the diversity climate survey at the workshop? What might Stephanie have done (or should she have been doing) in her supervisory role to most effectively manage what appears to be some diversity-related issues among her team? If you were Stephanie, in what post-workshop strategies might you engage to respond to the issues that emerged in the workshop? Do you think Stephanie's identity as an African American woman has anything to do with the issues that emerged at the workshop?

Discussion

Stephanie's Key Management and Supervisory Challenges. Larry Roper's chapter in this sourcebook discusses challenges and responsibilities as supervisors and managers with respect to helping staff navigate the complexities of working in a multicultural environment. In this case study, I use Roper's definition for the words diversity and multiculturalism. Roper defines diversity as "the ways in which people differ," and multiculturalism as "a person's capacity to successfully manage relationships and complex interactions with individuals from various cultures" (p. 72 of this sourcebook).

The background information in Case Study 4 suggests that Stephanie identified a number of challenges related to diversity and multiculturalism when she became the director of the student union. Two of these challenges were a student union staff that was not very diverse, and the perception on campus that the Student Center was a hangout for only certain groups of students. In addressing these two challenges, Stephanie made the case to her staff that the Center should be a place where all students at the institution feel welcome. Stephanie shares with her supervisees her belief that one approach to ensure that all students feel welcome in the Center is to make sure the staff of the Center reflects the diversity of the student community.

Given the information in the case study about student perceptions of the Center, do you concur with Stephanie's response that hiring a more diverse staff is the solution? Why or why not? What might be some other ideas for Stephanie to pursue to help change the perception of the Center in the minds of students?

The other challenge that has seemed to emerge for Stephanie in implementing her strategy to hire a more diverse staff is that some of the supervisees do not appear to be in agreement with Stephanie's emphasis on diversity. Also, supervisees appear to have differing perspectives about the emphasis placed on diversity within the Center.

Strategies for Multicultural Supervision. Based on the case study narrative, the conflicting perceptions among staff about diversity issues in the Center seem to have come to a head at the diversity workshop.

What do you think might be some of the underlying reasons for the breakdown of the diversity discussion at the workshop?

Roper says, "Effective supervisors should be able to build a work group that demonstrates support for the individual differences of members while at the same time developing a strong sense of community"(p. 127 in this sourcebook). Roper also states that "Whenever individuals gather for the purpose of work, there is a potential for power discrepancies to emerge" (p. 126 in this sourcebook).

The case study presented does not go into any detail about what work Stephanie has done with the individual members of her team to affirm their unique perspectives and the value that each has for the work of the Center. Other than the mention that the diversity workshop was suggested as one of the Center's professional development activities, the case study does not describe ways in which Stephanie has worked with supervisees to develop a sense of community among themselves.

What is your perspective regarding Roper's suggestion of the keys to successful multicultural supervision? If you were Stephanie, what might you have done to focus on both the individual and community aspects of multicultural supervision?

NEW DIRECTIONS FOR STUDENT SERVICES • DOI: 10.1002/ss

Post-Workshop Strategies for Stephanie. The case study uses the word *disaster* to describe the student union's professional development workshop on diversity. However, the issues that emerged from the workshop with respect to staff perspectives regarding diversity uncovered information for Stephanie about which she might otherwise not have been aware. As such, there is an opportunity for Stephanie to rethink her strategy for the implementation of what she believes is an important priority on diversity for the Center.

In emphasizing multiculturalism in my various supervisory roles, I have experienced challenges similar to Stephanie's. Based on my experience, I offer the following strategies for fostering multiculturalism in the workplace:

1. Assess organizational culture. As a supervisor, I found that before making changes that affect, or are affected by, the organizational culture, I need to make sure staff members feel that they have had the opportunity to participate in discussions about, and help shape, the change. Since staff members are likely to have different perspectives about the organizational culture, some type of assessment of the organization may be necessary. The goal of an organizational assessment is to provide all staff with a similar baseline of information about the organization.

There are many ways of conducting an organizational assessment. One assessment I utilize is a SWOT (strengths, weaknesses, opportunities, and threats) analysis. As part of the SWOT analysis, staff evaluate an organization's strengths and weaknesses and identify where the organization may find opportunities and threats. I particularly like the SWOT analysis technique because it invites the participation of many different stakeholders. The SWOT analysis is one method a supervisor might use to identify changes an organization may need to make toward achieving particular organizational goals.

What if Stephanie had engaged in SWOT analysis or some other assessment strategy to evaluate aspects of the student center and diversity had emerged as an issue of concern? In what way, if any, might such an assessment have helped Stephanie work with her team to make changes in the Center in response to the assessment?

2. Align discussions about diversity and multiculturalism with institutional mission. As a vice president for student affairs, I am charged with supporting my university's mission and strategic goals. In each of the six universities where I have worked, the university mission and/or its strategic goals focused on recruiting and retaining diverse student, staff, and faculty populations. In conversations with my staff about the importance of a focus on diversity and multiculturalism within the Division of Student Affairs, I make every effort to tie our student affairs goals in these areas to the overall university mission and strategic plan. Doing so helps staff understand that there are institutional reasons for divisional priorities. If the university where Stephanie serves as director of the student union has a focus on diversity as part of the institutional mission, Stephanie may have found more staff receptivity to her ideas explicitly linking any diversity-related goals for the Student Center to her institution's mission.

What does your institutional mission say about diversity? In what ways might you use your institutional mission (whether or not diversity is explicitly mentioned) to facilitate a conversation with your supervisees about diversity in your department?

3. *Engage in fierce conversations.* *Fierce Conversations* is the title of a book by Susan Scott (2002, 2004). Scott defines a fierce conversation as "one in which we come out from behind ourselves into the conversation and make it real" (p. 7). Scott's premise is that organizations, and teams within organizations, are most productive if the individual members of the organization are engaged in honest, authentic conversations in which each individual commits to sharing who they really are and what they really think, is fully engaged in communicating for mutual understanding, and is willing to tackle any of the tough challenges that are getting in the way of the organization's ability to accomplish its goals.

My current team had many challenges trying to be authentic in our conversations with one another. In addition to differences with respect to race, gender, and ethnicity, one of our most challenging areas of difference was the length of time each member of the team had worked at the university. Our team had an almost even split between those who had worked at the university ten years or more and those who had worked at the university five years or less.

Roper's point mentioned earlier in this chapter about the power dynamics that can emerge when a diverse group of individuals tries to work together was certainly true for my team. Within my team, it seemed that these dynamics got in the way during many of our conversations regarding how to tackle a variety of divisional challenges. Through a series of retreats with an outside consultant, my group learned that we needed to develop our abilities to communicate more effectively with one another and, more important, what skills we needed to develop to engage in *fierce conversations* as a means of understanding and working through our diverse perspectives and viewpoints.

In Case Study 3, the conversation among the staff about diversity does not go very well. The case study indicates that one of the reasons the diversity workshop did not go well was a poor workshop facilitator. I have shared an example of my own team's challenges with communication and our work to develop better communication techniques in our interpersonal relationships with one another as a way to offer another perspective on what might have been helpful for Stephanie's group in preparation for the diversity workshop. While the case study does not provide information on the preparation of Stephanie's team prior to the workshop, to what extent do you think a focus on developing communication techniques might have influenced the student union's diversity workshop?

4. *Supervisors understand their own multiculturalism.* In Chapter 7, Roper underscores that supervisors can position themselves well to supervise diverse staff by "understanding their own personal experiences and how those experiences affect the supervisor's ability to interact with others in ways that allow the other person to feel respected" (p. 123 in this sourcebook). Roper also states, "It is not unusual that a supervisor may be keenly aware of some aspects of diversity, yet be unable to discern the presence of other forms of diversity"(p. 122 in this sourcebook). As supervisors, we must critically assess our own strengths and limitations with regard to diversity and multiculturalism. For example, in what way does our particular background—for example, mine as an African American woman—influence how we view others? Are there some differences with which we are more comfortable than others?

Because Stephanie is an African American female, and the case study indicates she has hired and promoted a number of staff of color, might some members of her staff perceive race to be Stephanie's primary diversity focus? And if some staff view Stephanie as primarily focused on racial diversity, might some staff perceive that they are not included, or do not have a role, in the team's discussion about diversity?

What additional information about Stephanie could the case study have provided to help you assess Stephanie's multiculturalism in her role as a supervisor? How have you assessed and enhanced your own multiculturalism? How does your particular cultural background and/or demographic profile enhance or limit your perspective on multiculturalism?

Case Study 4

What if I supervise a consistently underperforming employee?

You are an assistant dean of student life and have an underperforming employee. Rita is currently an administrative assistant who is not very detail oriented, though she brings great enthusiasm to the job. The students who hang out in the office love her. In fact, Rita has recently received an outstanding service award from the student government. In your conversations with Rita regarding your concerns about her performance, you have also tried to encourage Rita to pursue other positions you think might be a better fit for her skills. Unfortunately, Rita seems to have no interest in pursuing other job opportunities, nor is her work getting any better.

Reflection Questions. What are a supervisor's responsibilities when a supervisee is underperforming? What are some strategies in which a supervisor might engage to help a supervisee improve her performance? What happens if a supervisee's work does not seem to be improving? How might the fact that Rita is well liked by students complicate your decision about what to do about Rita?

Discussion

Responsibilities of Supervisor for Underperforming Supervisees. Dalton's (2003) *Managing Human Resources* provides a helpful perspective on one's responsibilities as a supervisor of an underperforming supervisee. One focus of Dalton's conceptual framework is the responsibilities of managers in student affairs to hold supervisees accountable for the work they have been hired to do. Part of that accountability is making sure that supervisees have the training, support, and resources necessary to appropriately perform their jobs.

My definition of accountability is expecting the staff you supervise to perform the responsibilities delineated in their job descriptions. Also, accountability means staff performance will be evaluated based on the extent to which they meet those job responsibilities.

As a supervisor, how do you (or might you) communicate and enforce accountability standards with the staff you supervise? What does this definition of accountability mean in terms of your responsibilities as Rita's supervisor? How might you have approached the accountability and training/support aspects of supervision when you hired Rita?

A supervisee's job performance can be affected by any number of factors, including poorly defined job expectations, inadequate supervision, conflict between coworkers, off-the-job challenges (for example, family or financial problems, illness), or not having the requisite skills or passion for the position. This case study implies that, as Rita's supervisor, you do not believe the administrative assistant position is a good fit for her.

What is your assessment of Rita's fit for the administrative assistant position she currently holds? In what ways might you evaluate fit in your interview process for prospective applicants to positions in your department?

This case study implies that Rita has other positive qualities. She is enthusiastic and is well liked by the students who frequent the office. While Rita's lack of attention to detail is not an asset in her role as an administrative assistant, the skills that she does have may serve her well, or be a better fit, in a different position. As Rita's supervisor, your primary role is to work with Rita toward success in the administrative assistant position. It should not be your role to help find Rita another position you think might be a better fit for her. If you think Rita has skills that might be more applicable in other areas of the university (or even other non-university-related positions), there may be other approaches to working with Rita that you might consider. For example, you might help Rita identify her strengths and evaluate those strengths against her current job description and other jobs she indicates she might be interested in pursuing.

What Happens If a Supervisee's Work Does Not Seem to Be Improving? In the mid-level management class discussions, the class participants felt they needed more information and training about what to do as a supervisor when supervisory strategies do not help a supervisee improve. At what point in the supervision process does one consider firing an employee for poor performance?

Dalton (2003) believes that firing employees is something that student affairs professionals, in particular, have difficulty doing. According to Dalton:

> Student Affairs administrators have a plethora of euphemisms for the term "firing." We "terminate" employees, "let them go," "non-renew" their con-tracts, and "give them notice," but seldom do we "fire" them. The truth is that higher education administrators and student affairs administrators in particular have great difficulty firing employees. (p. 416)

Do you agree with Dalton's belief that firing staff is something that student affairs professionals find to be particularly challenging, or might this be something that any supervisor, regardless of the profession, has dif-ficulty doing? If you concur with Dalton, why do you think this is the case for student affairs professionals?

I agree with Dalton that student affairs supervisors appear to have dif-ficulty firing staff. I believe that many student affairs supervisors are uncomfortable firing employees because of our perception of ourselves as helping, caring, professionals. Think about the words we often use to describe our work as student affairs professionals—we *help, advise, counsel,* and *develop* others. As such, we avoid engaging in behaviors we perceive as contrary to those professional values. In a supervisory capacity, we see fir-ing as both a supervisee's failure to perform and our own failure to act in ways that we believe are in concert with the ways in which we define the work of our profession.

At what point in the process of supervising an underperforming employee should firing become an option to consider? In my experience, there is no hard-and-fast time line for determining at what point to fire an employee for poor performance. The human resources department at your institution can help you determine the particular steps you need to take, within the institution's protocol, to fire an employee for poor performance.

Given the information provided in Case Study 4, do you think the situation has risen to the level where termination should be considered? What additional information and other considerations would influence your decision as to whether Rita should be fired? If you think you might have to fire a staff member, do you know what the process is at your insti-tution for doing so?

What Happens If You Have to Fire Someone? The human resources department at your campus will be your best resource for working through the process once you decide you must fire a supervisee. In most instances there are many steps a supervisor must go through before the decision to fire an employee can be acted upon. However, sometimes a long process is necessary to ensure that performance problems are adequately documented, the employee is treated fairly, and the employee has been given adequate opportunity to improve her performance. Your institution's human resources office will also want to make sure that you follow all of the institutional and legal requirements related to an individual's rights as an employee.

A student in the midlevel management class asked, "But what if I have to actually sit down with one of my staff members and tell them that they are fired; how do I learn how to do that?" Your human resources department is again your best resource in this regard. As a midlevel manager, it is likely that both your human resources staff and your immediate supervisor will be part of any meeting with an employee you wish to terminate. Some human resources departments advise or require, depending on the circumstances and classification of the employee (union or nonunion represented), that you not participate in the termination meeting. Should you find yourself in a situation where you need to inform an employee that she is fired, some guideline for constructing the termination conversation, in addition to any assistance offered to you by your human resources department, can be found at the following Web sites:

The Right Way to Fire Someone, http://www.entrpreneur.com/article/166644
How to Fire an Employee, http://www.howtofireanemployee.net/

Please note that these two Web articles are offered as reference material only. Should you reach the point at which you must terminate an employee, you must follow your HR policies precisely, as they require.

Conclusion

This chapter provided four scenarios to allow you to explore various challenges that supervisors might encounter. Through reading and discussing the case studies included in this chapter, I hope you had the opportunity to think more deeply about how to approach your supervisory experience; how to respond if an ethical issue arises in your supervision of a staff member; how to manage in a multicultural environment; and what to do with an underperforming employee. The perspective I offered, related to each case study, is but one point of view. Hopefully, the reflection questions embedded in each case study stimulated your thinking about other approaches to each of the case studies presented.

The most important lesson I have learned in my many years as a senior manager in student affairs is, there is no one "right" way to approach supervision. However, there are some general supervisory principles with respect to communication of your supervisory expectations and holding staff accountable for those expectations: a strong commitment to ethical behavior for yourself and those you supervise, awareness of your own multiculturalism and how your particular multicultural perspective enhances or limits your supervisory style and priorities, and the obligation supervisors have to ensure that supervisees perform well and have access to the professional development opportunities.

Supervision is both a challenge and a gift. Being a supervisor means one is accountable for the performance of others and the achievement of organizational outcomes. In exercising accountability the supervisor must deal with issues such as staff conflict, underperformance, and changes in organizational dynamics (for example, budget shortfalls, senior leadership changes, federal mandates), among others. At the same time, as a supervisor, one has the opportunity to nurture the growth and development of supervisees, to demonstrate commitment to the success of others, and invest in helping supervisees achieve their aspirations. As you read this chapter, I hope you were able to gain insight on how you might confront the challenges that come your way, while also seeing in each case where you could be a positive force on behalf of the supervisee's success and well-being.

References

Dalton, J. "Managing Human Resources." In D. B. Woodard (ed.), *Student Services: A Handbook for the Profession* (pp. 397–417). San Francisco: Jossey-Bass, 2003.

Renn, K. A., & Hodges, H. P. "The First Year on the Job: Experiences of New Professionals in Student Affairs." *NASPA Journal*, 2007, 44(2), 367–391.

Reybold, L. E., Halx, M. D., and Jimenez, A. L. (2008). "Professional Integrity in Higher Education: A Study of Administrative Staff Ethics in Student Affairs." *Journal of College Student Development*, 49(2), 110–124.

Scott, S. *Fierce Conversations*. New York: Berkley Publishing Group, 2002, 2004.

Stock-Ward, S. R., and Javorek, M. E. "Applying Theory to Practice: Supervision in Student Affairs." *NASPA Journal*, 2003, 40(3), 77–92.

Sundberg, D. C., & Fried, J. (1997). "Ethical Dialogues on Campus." In J. Fried (ed.), New Directions for Student Services, No. 77. *Ethics for Today's Campus: New Perspectives on Education, Student Development, and Institutional Management* (pp. 67–79). San Francisco: Jossey-Bass. Retrieved October 3, 2011, from Wiley Online Library.

Wilcox, J. R., & Ebbs, S. L. (1992). *The Leadership Compass: Values and Ethics in Higher Education*. Washington, DC: The George Washington University.

Winston, R. B., Jr, & Creamer, D. G. (1998). "Staff Supervision and Professional Development: An Integrated Approach." In W. A. Bryan and R. A. Schwartz (eds.), *Strategies for Staff Development: Personal and Professional Education in the 21st century* (pp. 29–42). New Directions for Student Services, No. 84. San Francisco: Jossey-Bass. Retrieved October 3, 2011, from Wiley Online Library.

LORI S. WHITE *is vice president for student affairs at Southern Methodist University.*

INDEX

Statement of Ownership

Statement of Ownership, Management, and Circulation (required by 39 U.S.C. 3685), filed on OCTOBER 1, 2011 for NEW DIRECTIONS FOR STUDENT SERVICES (Publication No. 0164-7970), published Quarterly for an annual subscription price of $89 at Wiley Subscription Services, Inc., at Jossey-Bass, One Montgomery St., Suite 1200, San Francisco, CA 94104-4594.

The names and complete mailing addresses of the Publisher, Editor, and Managing Editor are: Publisher, Wiley Subscription Services, Inc., A Wiley Company at San Francisco, One Montgomery St., Suite 1200, San Francisco, CA 94104-4594; Editor, Elizabeth J. Whitt, Editor in Chief, 221 North Grand, DB 450, Saint Louis University, St. Louis, MO 63103; Managing Editor, None,   . Contact Person: Joe Schuman; Telephone: 415-782-3232.

NEW DIRECTIONS FOR STUDENT SERVICES is a publication owned by Wiley Subscription Services, Inc., 111 River St., Hoboken, NJ 07030. The known bondholders, mortgagees, and other security holders owning or holding 1% or more of total amount of bonds, mortgages, or other securities are (see list).

	Average No. Copies Each Issue During Preceding 12 Months	No. Copies Of Single Issue Published Nearest To Filing Date (Summer 2011)
15a. Total number of copies (net press run)	870	837
15b. Legitimate paid and/or requested distribution (by mail and outside mail)		
15b(1). Individual paid/requested mail subscriptions stated on PS form 3541 (include direct written request from recipient, telemarketing, and Internet requests from recipient, paid subscriptions including nominal rate subscriptions, advertiser's proof copies, and exchange copies)	254	233
15b(2). Copies requested by employers for distribution to employees by name or position, stated on PS form 3541	0	0
15b(3). Sales through dealers and carriers, street vendors, counter sales, and other paid or requested distribution outside USPS	0	0
15b(4). Requested copies distributed by other mail classes through USPS	0	0
15c. Total paid and/or requested circulation (sum of 15b(1), (2), (3), and (4))	254	233
15d. Nonrequested distribution (by mail and outside mail)		
15d(1). Outside county nonrequested copies stated on PS form 3541	39	38
15d(2). In-county nonrequested copies stated on PS form 3541	0	0
15d(3). Nonrequested copies distributed through the USPS by other classes of mail	0	0
15d(4). Nonrequested copies distributed outside the mail	0	0
15e. Total nonrequested distribution (sum of 15d(1), (2), (3), and (4))	39	38
15f. Total distribution (sum of 15c and 15e)	293	271
15g. Copies not distributed	577	566
15h. Total (sum of 15f and 15g)	870	837
15i. Percent paid and/or requested circulation (15c divided by 15f times 100)	86.9%	85.9%

I certify that all information furnished on this form is true and complete. I understand that anyone who furnishes false or misleading information on this form or who omits material or information requested on this form may be subject to criminal sanctions (including fines and imprisonment) and/or civil sanctions (including civil penalties).

Statement of Ownership will be printed in the Winter 2011 issue of this publication.

(signed) Susan E. Lewis, VP & Publisher-Periodicals

NEW DIRECTIONS FOR STUDENT SERVICES

ORDER FORM SUBSCRIPTION AND SINGLE ISSUES

DISCOUNTED BACK ISSUES:

Use this form to receive 20% off all back issues of *New Directions for Student Services*.
All single issues priced at **$23.20** (normally $29.00)

TITLE   ISSUE NO.   ISBN

_____   _____   _____
_____   _____   _____
_____   _____   _____

Call 888-378-2537 or see mailing instructions below. When calling, mention the promotional code JBNND
to receive your discount. For a complete list of issues, please visit www.josseybass.com/go/ndss

SUBSCRIPTIONS: (1 YEAR, 4 ISSUES)

☐ New Order   ☐ Renewal

U.S.	☐ Individual: $89	☐ Institutional: $275
CANADA/MEXICO	☐ Individual: $89	☐ Institutional: $315
ALL OTHERS	☐ Individual: $113	☐ Institutional: $349

Call 888-378-2537 or see mailing and pricing instructions below.
Online subscriptions are available at www.onlinelibrary.wiley.com

ORDER TOTALS:

Issue / Subscription Amount: $ _____

Shipping Amount: $ _____
(for single issues only – subscription prices include shipping)

Total Amount: $ _____

SHIPPING CHARGES:

First Item $6.00
Each Add'l Item $2.00

(No sales tax for U.S. subscriptions. Canadian residents, add GST for subscription orders. Individual rate subscriptions must
be paid by personal check or credit card. Individual rate subscriptions may not be resold as library copies.)

BILLING & SHIPPING INFORMATION:

☐ **PAYMENT ENCLOSED:** *(U.S. check or money order only. All payments must be in U.S. dollars.)*

☐ **CREDIT CARD:** ☐ VISA ☐ MC ☐ AMEX

Card number _____ Exp. Date_____

Card Holder Name_____ Card Issue # _____

Signature _____ Day Phone_____

☐ **BILL ME:** *(U.S. institutional orders only. Purchase order required.)*

Purchase order # _____
Federal Tax ID 13559302 • GST 89102-8052

Name_____

Address_____

Phone_____ E-mail_____

Copy or detach page and send to: **John Wiley & Sons, One Montgomery Street, Suite 1200,**
                                     San Francisco, CA 94104-4594

Order Form can also be faxed to: **888-481-2665**

PROMO JBNND